Education and Equality

Education

nd Equality

DANIELLE ALLEN

With comments by

TOMMIE SHELBY,

MARCELO SUÁREZ-OROZCO,

MICHAEL REBELL, *and*

QUIARA ALEGRÍA HUDES

THE UNIVERSITY OF CHICAGO PRESS

Chicago and London

Danielle Allen is director of the Edmond J. Safra Center for Ethics and professor of government and education at Harvard University. The recipient of a MacArthur Fellowship, she is the author of many books, including, most recently, Our Declaration, and coeditor of From Voice to Influence and Education, Justice, and Democracy, the latter two published by the University of Chicago Press.

The University of Chicago Press, Chicago 60637
The University of Chicago Press, Ltd., London
© 2016 by The University of Chicago
All rights reserved. Published 2016.
Printed in the United States of America

25 24 23 22 21 20 19 18 17 16   1 2 3 4 5

ISBN-13: 978-0-226-37310-2 (cloth)
ISBN-13: 978-0-226-37324-9 (e-book)
DOI: 10.7208/chicago/9780226373249.001.0001

Library of Congress Cataloging-in-Publication Data

Names: Allen, Danielle S., 1971– author. | Shelby, Tommie, 1967– | Suárez-Orozco, Marcelo M., 1956– | Rebell, Michael A. | Hudes, Quiara Alegría.
Title: Education and equality / Danielle Allen ; with comments by Tommie Shelby, Marcelo Suárez-Orozco, Michael Rebell, and Quiara Alegría Hudes.
Description: Chicago : The University of Chicago Press, 2016. | Includes bibliographical references and index.
Identifiers: LCCN 2015041273| ISBN 9780226373102 (cloth : alk. paper) | ISBN 9780226373249 (e-book)
Subjects: LCSH: Educational equalization—United States. | Education—United States. | Education—Philosophy.
Classification: LCC LC213.2 .A55 2016 | DDC 379.2/6—dc23 LC record available at http://lccn.loc.gov /2015041273

♾ This paper meets the requirements of ANSI/NISO Z39.48-1992 (Permanence of Paper).

CONTENTS

ACKNOWLEDGMENTS

My thanks first of all to Stanford's Tanner Lecture Committee, which gave me the opportunity to wrestle to the ground a question that had been plaguing me for some time. My thanks, too, to the many wonderful people who hosted me in Palo Alto, including Rob Reich, Josh Ober, Josh Cohen, and Joanie Berry. My collaborators for the volume *Education, Justice, and Democracy* provided the first context for the development of this argument. I am very grateful to them for their input on its early versions; Tony Laden, Harry Brighouse, and Adam Swift made especially significant contributions. Of course, the audiences at the lectures and my four brilliant commentators, whose remarks are included here, made the occasion what it was and gave me the most challenging, most intense, most rewarding three-day intellectual experience of my life. Truly it's a blessing to have the chance to have one's work read and responded to by such extraordinarily thoughtful, generous, imaginative, and tough-minded readers. Quiara Alegría Hudes's comment brought me to tears on the occasion. Thanks are due next to those who went above and beyond with helpful commentary and guidance when I asked them to read the written version of the lectures: Charles Payne, Glen Weyl, and Leo Casey. Peter Levine, who read the manuscript for the press, and an additional anonymous reviewer offered equally incisive commentary. An invitation from Henry Farrell to comment on Thomas Piketty's *Capital in the 21st Century* for Crooked Timber helped me clean up some aspects of my thinking. My colleagues in the School of Social Science at the Institute for Advanced Study (IAS) from 2007 to 2015 have lived with this work and in closer proximity to it than anyone else and have provided a superb intellectual environment for its coming to completion. I can imagine nowhere else where I could have had the time and range of interlocutors to assimilate the diversity of literatures that was necessary for me to write these lectures. My great thanks, then, to Joan Scott, Michael Walzer, Eric Maskin, Didier Fassin, and Dani Rodrik, as well as to the two directors of the institute who supported this work enthusiastically, Peter Goddard and Robbert Djikgraaf. My Humanities and Liberal Arts Assessment (HULA) research team—Maggie Schein, Sheena Kang, Chris Pupik Dean, Melanie Webb, and Annie Walton-

Doyle—are a terrific set of intellectual partners. The excellent staff in the School of Social Science at IAS was also indispensable: Donne Petito, Linda Garat, Nancy Cotterman, and of course, my remarkable assistant, Laura McCune. Thanks without measure go to my father, William Allen, who gave me the phrase "humanistic baseline." Finally, my greatest debt is to Jimmy, Nora, and William Doyle, who have had to tolerate too many absences and who are always, blissfully, the reason that it would be better to be home.

CHAPTER 1] Two Concepts of Education

INTRODUCTION: THE PROBLEM

We are currently awash in torrents of public conversation about education. As of early September 2014, Randi Weingarten, president of the American Federation of Teachers, had 42,400 tweets to her name. For the period between September 2013 and September 2014, the *New York Times* archive generates 178,000 "articles on education." And education is among Americans' top ten political concerns out of a list of some thirty-five issues.[1] There is so much talk about education that one can't help but think that perhaps the most sensible thing to do would be just to get on with it: to quit conversing and get back to teaching. In other words, this book and I are perhaps part of some kind of problem, not a solution.

Aside from their sheer volume, the other notable feature of our countless public conversations about education is how many of them have to do with equality. In 2009, former house speaker Newt Gingrich and black civil rights activist Reverend Al Sharpton famously joined up for a public tour to advocate educational reform. They identified problems in education as the civil rights issue of our time. Similarly, our many public conversations about income inequality inevitably turn to the topic of education. Thus, the French economist Thomas Piketty, in his book *Capital* (2014), writes, "Historical experience suggests that the principal mechanism for convergence [of incomes] at the international as well as the domestic level is the diffusion of knowledge. In other words, the poor catch up with the rich to the extent that they achieve the same level of technological know-how, skill, and education."[2] He is not the first to make this point. The influential US economists Claudia Goldin and Larry Katz do as well, for instance, in their book *The Race between Education and Technology*.

Here, too, I must count myself as part of this problem—or, if it is not a "problem," then at least part of the phenomenon of a durable societal obsession with "education" and "equality."[3] For nearly five years now, I've been going around giving lectures under the title "Education and Equality." I haven't, however, been plowing a single furrow. My arguments have constantly shifted. My experience has been that of pursuing a highly elusive object of analysis; an adequate framework for thinking about the relationship between education and equality has felt always just beyond reach.

Over the course of my constant scrutiny of this topic, I have made normative arguments that ideal educational institutions in a democratic society ought to lift the educational level of the entire population as high as possible while also making it possible for those with special gifts to achieve the highest heights of intellectual and creative excellence and simultaneously ensuring that the pathways to those highest heights can be entered into by anyone from any social position. Imagine a western mesa, but one that has peaks like the Rockies jutting out of it, with trailheads for the ascent of each peak marked plainly and boldly.[4]

I have also made policy arguments. For instance, I make the case that the achievement of such an ideal requires reforming our approaches to zoning and municipal policy;[5] committing public funding to early childhood education, community colleges, and public universities;[6] distributing admission tickets to elite colleges and universities by means of geographic lotteries over a certain basic threshold of achievement;[7] constructing tuition and aid policies based on transparency about what any given institution actually spends on educating a student;[8] and broadly disseminating the competencies, aptitudes, and skills necessary to convert social relationships that are currently costly—namely, those that bridge boundaries of social difference—into relationships that bring mutual benefit.[9]

Yet, for all the pages and PowerPoint slides, I do not feel that I have been able to come to a resting point in my account of the relationship between education and equality. With this book, and the responses from commentators, I am hoping to put this insistent intellectual problem to bed at last.

Why exactly is it so hard to think about education and equality in relation to each other? There is, of course, the fact that equality is simply a difficult concept to talk about. I often find that students think that to say two things are "equal" is to say that they are "the same." But, of course, "equal" and "same" are not synonyms. To be the same is to be identical. But to be equal is to have an equivalent degree of some specific quality or attribute in comparison to someone else. To talk about equality, one must always begin by asking, "Equal to whom and in what respect?"

Importantly, the effective use of a concept of equality in a sociopolitical context requires that one pinpoint whether the discussion pertains to human equality, political equality, social equality, or economic equality. Or perhaps, in place of the last, one will replace an ideal of economic equality with an ideal of economic justice, or fairness, or opportunity. Then there are relations among each of these types of equality. I think clarifying those relationships is among the most important tasks of political philosophy, particularly in our present moment. Yet when we invoke the concept of equality in our conversations about education, for the most part, we don't bother to define what we actually mean by it or to identify which aspect of human experience we wish to pick out for analysis.[10]

Beyond the simple fact that we often leave the idea of equality unspecified in our conversations about educational policy, another issue, too, stirs up my vague unease with how we commonly invoke the concept in these discussions. The quotation from Piketty's *Capital* that I quoted just a moment ago is revealing. Let me repeat a bit of it again: "In other words, the poor catch up with the rich to the extent that they achieve the same level of technological know-how, skill, and education."[11] Note that the problem that education is here used to solve is that of poverty or, at least, of unequal income and/or wealth distribution. This tracks our most common way of discussing equality in relation to education. Discussions of educational reform are very often proxies for conversations about poverty, and insofar as this is the case, it is often unclear how much the conversation actually concerns education itself.

Similarly, if one returns to my normative picture and policy prescriptions—the mesa with its peaks and the policies about funding, admission, and municipal planning—you will find that the picture I have painted is entirely about the egalitarian *funding* and *allocation* or *distribution* of some *good* called education, but not particularly about whatever the actual good called education fundamentally is. In other words, for all our talk about education and equality, we don't actually talk very much about how education in itself relates to equality, regardless of whether the equality we have in mind is human, political, social, or connected to economic fairness.

This brings me to the basic problem that motivates this book. I think that education itself—a practice of human development—has, intrinsic to the practice, important contributions to make to the defense of human equality, to the cultivation of political and social equality, and to the emergence of fair economic orders. But I think we have lost sight of just how education in itself—putting aside questions of funding and distribution—relates to those egalitarian concerns. When I say "putting aside questions of funding and distribution," I do not mean that those issues are irrelevant. To the contrary, they have powerful impacts on educational outcomes and on the degree to which we achieve social and political equality and economic egalitarianism. Yet, in focusing as consistently as we do on these topics, we have actually lost our ability to see other features of education that are relevant to the topic of equality. If we are to do right by the students we purport to educate, in whatever context and at whatever level, I think we need to recover that vision. Consequently, my goal for this book is to effect a recovery of our understanding of just how education and equality are intrinsically connected to each other. Achieving this recovery will not negate the force of socioeconomic factors on the degree to which education supports egalitarian social outcomes, but it should provide us additional resources for combatting the powerful influence of those factors.

Here is the plan for what follows. First, I begin with some conceptual cleanup work. Drawing on the mid-twentieth-century philosophers John Rawls and Hannah Arendt, I hope to secure some basic conceptual architecture for thinking about education. This will establish what I call a "humanistic baseline" for understanding what education is. This cleaned-up understanding of education should help clarify our conversations about our goals for both schooling and higher education. This will be the main work of this first chapter, and I will wrap it up by examining just how a humanistic baseline for understanding the meaning of education might help us reframe key policy questions.

In my second chapter, I will turn to the specific policy domain that appears most freshly lit by my account. This is the domain that many people refer to as "civic education." I argue that we should reorient ourselves to a concept of "participatory readiness," and I will lay out a proposed framework for thinking about the desirable content of a new approach to cultivating such participatory readiness. This participatory readiness is actually of critical relevance to other egalitarian concerns, including economic ones, and I will suggest that the cultivation of participatory readiness probably depends fundamentally on the humanistic aspects of the curriculum. In other words, the identification of the humanistic baseline for establishing a justification for education will turn out to have in fact provided a foundation for a defense of the humanities, as well as the beginnings of an explanation for how education in itself has egalitarian potential. This means, of course, that the fate of the humanities and the fate of so-called civic education are likely to rise and fall together.

In sum, the task of this book is to clarify our understanding of education, its intrinsic connection to equality, and the relevance of the study of the humanities to education's intrinsic egalitarian potentialities.

TWO CONCEPTS OF EDUCATION:
THE VOCATIONAL VERSUS THE LIBERAL?

For all the talk about education in contemporary culture, do we actually have an adequate framework for defining what it is? As an object of anthropological and sociological analysis, education is a relative newcomer. Although the French sociologist Émile Durkheim and African American sociologist W. E. B. DuBois launched the sociology of education in the late nineteenth century, sustained interest did not emerge until after World War II, when the field of the anthropology of education came into its own. The late inclusion of education among the practices that an anthropologist or sociologist might study reflects the fact that many of the earliest templates for these disciplines—the work of nineteenth-century scholars like Friedrich Engels, Karl Marx, Fustel de Coulanges, Henry Maine, and Max Weber—began from analyses of Western antiquity, where education was generally not an autonomous social practice but dependent on other social forms. For instance, in ancient Greece, religious ritual, legal practices, military training, and so on largely provided the context for training the young. Some ancients could conceive of education as an autonomous field of social practice—most notably the Greek philosophers Plato and Aristotle—but their anticipation of "systems of education" was largely unmatched in practice (although Sparta stands as an exception). In contrast, China's extensive network of formal educational institutions began its development in the third millennium BCE. Only once a social practice is autonomous—conducted through rituals or institutions built for the sake of that practice and no other—can it be said to have a logic and also a structure of action-guiding principles and rules that emerge from that logic.[12]

In addition to focusing on autonomous social practices, anthropologists and sociologists have sought to understand their conversion into sociopoliti-

cal practices. By this conversion, I mean the moment when legitimate public officials acquire authority over a practice that has previously been managed mostly by private individuals, as, for instance, when a society gives up
allowing individuals to effect retribution for wrongdoing through methods
of self-help and instead designates public authorities to manage responses to
wrongdoing. This is the moment when *social* practices of *revenge* instead become *sociopolitical* practices of *punishment*. In other words, at various points
in history, phenomena like revenge, mating, raiding, and possession of land
and other goods were co-opted by newly developing political realms and
turned into punishment, marriage, war, property, and markets. In the history of Western sociopolitical development, we can say that "revenge" had
become "punishment" by at least 800 BCE (although this transition occurred
more than once, not only in antiquity, but again in the medieval period).
Education did not undergo an equivalent conversion until well after antiquity had faded away.

The first versions of Western educational institutions were scribal training
centers in ancient Egypt and the ancient Near East and philosophical, rhetorical, and medical schools, as well as early schools for children, in Greece
and Rome.[13] Then, over the course of late antiquity and the Middle Ages, educational institutions took shape through the development of centers of religious training in the different monotheistic traditions, including the emergence of universities in Bologna, Paris, and Oxford in the eleventh century.[14]
The emergence of these institutions was followed by others: to pick out just
two examples, the establishment in England of schools for poor boys (for instance, the now extremely posh Winchester and Eton) as feeders to the new
universities and, during the Renaissance, the training of artists in the schools
of particular painters. But the processes by which political authorities established universal or compulsory education began in Europe only in the seven-
teenth century and in the United States were completed only in 1918, when
the last of the states then in the union made education up through the age of
sixteen compulsory.[15] As a consequence of the relatively late arrival in Western history of education as a fully autonomous sociopolitical practice on par
with punishment, economics, and war, scholars are still in the early stages of
coming to understand its logic.

Despite the relative youthfulness of education as a state practice, it might
seem, however, that our current public conversations about education do

not in fact evidence any confusion or uncertainty about the nature of education. This is one of the few areas of public policy where politicians from
either major party tend to say roughly the same thing. Both Democrats and
Republicans clearly articulate what could reasonably be called a neoliberal
educational agenda with a focus on educating the national population to
succeed in global market competition. Here is Barack Obama from the 2012
Democratic National Convention:

> I promise you, we can out-educate and out-compete any nation on
> Earth. Help me recruit 100,000 math and science teachers within ten
> years and improve early childhood education.
>
> Help give two million workers the chance to learn skills at their
> community college that will lead directly to a job. Help us work with
> colleges and universities to cut in half the growth of tuition costs over
> the next ten years. We can meet that goal together.
>
> You can choose that future for America.[16]

And here is Mitt Romney at the 2012 Republican National Convention:

> I am running for president to help create a better future. A future where
> everyone who wants a job can find one. Where no senior fears for the
> security of their retirement. An America where every parent knows that
> their child will get an education that leads them to a good job and a
> bright horizon.
>
> Second, we will give our fellow citizens the skills they need for the
> jobs of today and the careers of tomorrow. When it comes to the school
> your child will attend, every parent should have a choice, and every
> child should have a chance.[17]

The rhetorical affinities extend beyond the presidential campaign trail.
Both 2012 candidates echoed the language of the preamble to the bipartisan
Common Core State Standards for college and career readiness, which were
created and promoted by the National Governors Association. Here is a por-
tion of the preamble:

> The Common Core State Standards define the rigorous skills and
> knowledge in English Language Arts and Mathematics that need to
> be effectively taught and learned for students to be ready to succeed

academically in credit-bearing, college-entry courses and in workforce training programs. These standards have been developed to be:

Fewer, clearer, and higher, to best drive effective policy and practice;
Aligned with college and work expectations, so that all students are
*   prepared for success upon graduating from high school;*
Inclusive of rigorous content and applications of knowledge through
*   higher-order skills, so that all students are prepared for the 21st century;*
Internationally benchmarked, so that all students are prepared for
*   succeeding in our global economy and society; and*
Research and evidence-based.

The standards intend to set forward thinking goals for student performance based in evidence about what is required for success. The standards developed will set the stage for US education not just beyond next year, but for the next decade, and they must ensure *all* American students are prepared for the global economic workplace.[18]

In short, in this country, we seem to know just what we should be pursuing in education: college and career readiness as preparation for the global economy. Given that this goal is backed by state power generated by the richest and most powerful government the world has ever known, we have to take seriously the idea that this choice of goal is of considerable consequence for the future of our own culture at least.

What exactly is the cultural consequence of constructing an educational system around this goal of college and career readiness as preparation for the global economy? As our public conversations have unfolded, the reigning political ideology in education has generated the common critique that the orientation is overly "vocational." The story of how such a vocationally oriented frame of global competiveness came to dominate our public conversations about education is familiar. The Soviet launch of the first satellite in 1957 provoked a sense that this country was falling behind in a Cold War scientific contest. The response was the National Defense of Education Act, signed into law in 1958. Then, in 1983, the Reagan-era report "A Nation at Risk" further spurred the view that the United States was falling behind. Although its data were later debunked, it included provocative summary sentences such as, "If an unfriendly foreign power had attempted to impose on America the mediocre educational performance that exists today, we might well have viewed it as an act of war."[19] This report is generally understood to have kicked off the era of school reform that still shapes educational discussion and policy. And in 2007, the National Academy of Sciences put out a report called "Rising above the Gathering Storm," which emphasized the need for significant improvements in science and technology education and investment. The report's authors wrote, "An educated, innovative, motivated workforce—human capital—is the most precious resource of any country in this new, flat world. Yet there is widespread concern about our K–12 science and mathematics education system, the foundation of that human capital in today's global economy."[20] This influential report has impacted educational policy conversations, driving an increase of focus on STEM (science, technology, engineering, and mathematics) fields. We can see the impact in Obama's 2013 State of the Union address, when he announced a competition to "redesign America's high schools." Rewards would go, he said at the time, to schools that develop more classes "that focus on science, technology, engineering and math—the skills today's employers are looking for to fill jobs right now and in the future."[21]

Those who critique this educational vision typically invoke the "liberal arts" by way of contrast. Of course, a straightforward dichotomy between vocational and liberal learning is relevant mostly in the context of elite colleges and universities. As the cultural historian and literary scholar Louis Menand has argued, such campuses often suffer from "an allergy to the term 'vocational.'"[22] Nonetheless, the antithesis between "vocational" and "liberal" that has developed on college campuses structures our broader debates about the purposes of education, and these can come to feel stuck in a simple and endless tug of war between those two poles. Is the point of education enriching the life of the mind or securing a job?

Of course, it is both, and it is, in fact, possible to get past this blockage in public conversation.[23] We can do so by recognizing that our conversations about education have the shape that they do because we are operating with two different concepts of education. In the next section, I'd like to clarify those two concepts in order to lead us to a resolution of the seeming opposition between the vocational and the liberal arts conceptions of education.

A HUMANISTIC BASELINE

Readers who are philosophers will already know that in referring to "two concepts of education," I am riffing on the political philosopher John Rawls, who in 1955 published an important essay called "Two Concepts of Rules."[24] In this early paper, Rawls pointed out that the perpetual debates among penal theorists over whether the proper justification for punishment was deterrent (and therefore utilitarian) or retributive (and so based on a commonplace morality) stem from a failure to understand the logic of practices, of which punishment was one of his two examples (promise keeping was the other). He argued (following David Hume, Ludwig Wittgenstein, and John Austin) that for any given practice, there is a distinction between justifying a practice and justifying a particular action falling under it. As an example, there is a distinction between justifying punishment and justifying punishing. The first kind of justification requires answering the question, "Why does the state (generally) punish people?" The second kind of justification requires answering the question, "Why did the state punish that particular person?"

According to Rawls, the answer to the latter question requires a retributive statement, for instance: "That particular man was punished as a response to the wrong he had done and in proportion to that wrong." However, the answer to the question of why states generally punish may, again according to Rawls, be utilitarian. Take the following as an example: "In order to keep wrong-doing to a minimum by deterring would-be wrong-doers through the example of the punishments of others."[25] But Rawls's neat distinction obscures a few other important distinctions. When we ask, "Why does the state (generally) punish people?", we are in fact asking two questions: first, "Why has punishment come to exist as an institution that distinguishes human social organization from hives and galaxies?,"[26] and second, "Why is the state justified in operating institutions of punishment?" The first question seeks a causal explanation; the second question seeks a justification for state action.[27]

Take the game of baseball as an example. The emergence of the game as a social practice is *explained* by the goal of leisure. But the actions of individuals participating in the game — swinging at balls, running around bases, catching and throwing balls — are *justified* by the goal not of leisure but of scoring more runs than an opponent. And the actions of corporate actors who have co-opted the game of baseball to develop, for instance, a professional version of the sport are justified by the goal of profit. The goals that explain the emergence of a practice, the goals that justify the effort to regulate the practice, and the goals that justify actions undertaken within it are all logically separate; if they turn out to be the same, that coincidence is merely accidental. Thus, it can be a matter of social utility[28] that practices should arise and be co-opted by the state, for which the goals of the actions falling under them are not utilitarian but either moral or eudaemonistic. What do I mean by "eudaemonistic"? The term comes from the Greek word for "happiness" (*eudaimonia*) and designates an ethical outlook organized around the efforts of individuals to achieve their full human flourishing by means of the development of their internal capacities.

The case of education is like that of punishment. Analysts of education move in a perpetual circle when they argue over its proper justification — *economic* competitiveness, the development of *citizens*, or enablement of a eudaemonistic *human flourishing*. We need to recognize that, as with punishment, the logic of education makes two different kinds of justification relevant to the practice: there is the justification for the state's maintenance of a system of education and the justification for particular instances of teaching carried out within that system.

In order to draw out the point, let's consider the very different schools that emerged in different historical periods prior to the nationalization of education: in chronological order, scribal training centers; philosophical, medical, and rhetorical schools; theological programs; universities; and schools of artists. These educational institutions were founded for different reasons—for instance, scribal training centers to help rulers control their property and the flow of goods or religious training centers to prepare priests and theologians and thereby supply religious organizations with manpower. These different schools were thus directed toward diverse ends. But in terms of the activity that occurred within them, which allows them as institutions to be classified as fundamentally aimed at the same goal (namely, education), all shared the aspiration to direct the development of human capacities. While the institutions of formal education arise on the basis of diverse justifications, within these different institutions, the activity of educating and also the techniques developed to pursue teaching and learning are identified by a single end: cultivating human development. This is true even when a student chooses a vocational training course for the sake of making money. In order for that training to succeed, it must still affect the development of the student qua human being—for that is what it means for any of us to cultivate capacities and abilities. As Hunter Rawlings, the former president of Cornell and the University of Iowa, has eloquently put it, education "is the awakening of a human being."[29]

In our current context, then, it is entirely reasonable that the justification for the co-optation of education by the state, for the conversion of education into a sociopolitical practice, might be utilitarian—a state asserts authority over education as a matter of securing social reproduction. Achieving this requires economic and/or military competitiveness for the state and preservation of its state form; in the context of a democracy, the system-level justification for education therefore entails a twinned utilitarian concern about generating economic and/or military competitiveness and producing citizens prepared to maintain democratic life.[30] But the justification for the actions falling under the practice, particular instances of educating, the micro-level of justification, cannot be utilitarian.

What do I mean by that strong statement? Clearly, people do often provide utilitarian or more broadly consequentialist justifications for education. The point is that when they do so, they may indeed justify the state's involvement in institutions of education but they actually fail to justify the activity of educating as such. Economists, for instance, distinguish between the consumption and investment benefits of education, or between the intrinsic and extrinsic benefits. As Helen Ladd and Susanna Loeb put it, "Intrinsic benefits arise when education is valued for its own sake such as the pleasure of being able to solve a complex problem or appreciate artistic expression, and extrinsic benefits arise when education serves as an instrument for the attainment of other valued outcomes such the higher income for working parents that is facilitated by having children in school, or the potential for the recipients of education to seek higher paying jobs and fulfilling careers than would otherwise be possible."[31]

But when one scrutinizes the extrinsic benefits that are most often identified as flowing from education—higher paying jobs, for instance—one notices that education is only one means of achieving those ends. One might, for instance, also obtain a higher paying job through cronyism. These extrinsic ends might justify activities other than education; in no way do they necessarily justify education. In contrast, the goals that define education *as* education, and thereby provide its proper justification, must be goals that can be achieved only through education: these are goals of human development, pursued as such.

Our considered moral judgment, to crib from Rawls, is that the state of affairs where a person has been educated is better than if she has not been, and it is better for her own sake, regardless of any consequence of educating her. We recognize educating *as* educating, in its various forms, because in all cases, one party has undertaken to spur the positive human development of another, an awakening. Across the different examples of education, what counts as success is the activation in the student of positive capacities that had previously been latent. Moreover, we care about the activation of those capacities regardless of the consequences. We do not, for instance, cease educating the child who has cancer because she has cancer. This is not to say that the consequences that flow from activating latent human capacities are unimportant—just that those consequences do not themselves justify the activation.

The important point here is that even when a student pursues education as a means to moneymaking, she is choosing as her means an activity whose form is built around a different set of goals. Of course, as the ancient Greek philosopher Aristotle long ago pointed out, the ends of moneymaking and of human flourishing are not separate from one another. In order to achieve a broad eudaemonistic human flourishing, we also need the means to live. Close attention to the logic of education reveals any strong distinction between utilitarian and eudaemonistic goals to be overdrawn. Similarly, even if one thinks it necessary to teach a child his tribe's rituals in order to preserve that tribe (a collective utilitarian concern), one in all probability also thinks that life in that tribe is in the child's best interest (a eudaemonistic perspective), so one's view about inculcating social norms is tethered to a view about the child's good. An educational system is constituted by a multitude of particular actions that involve the relation between teachers and students, where each student must always be an end in himself, not a means to some other end. When we try to cultivate good teachers, we seek to instill this instinct. This effort flows from the moral intuition that the appropriate justification for the actual activity of educating is a broad eudaemonism, not social utility.

Rawls's neat distinction, then, between the justification for rules that structure practices and the justification for rules that structure the activities conducted in the context of that practice helps us see that thinking about education requires us to think on two levels. We therefore need to understand when each level of justification is relevant. It is reasonable to think about social utility and about how a whole educational system might achieve social utility. It may even be necessary to do that.[32] But the justification for particular instances of educating must instead be eudaemonistic. What we are thinking about as education won't count as such unless we also think about it from the perspective of the individual being educated. In order to count as education, the practices sponsored by those institutions need to further the development of an individual qua human being—namely, a creature whose flourishing entails the development of a range of valuable cognitive, affective, and intersubjective capacities. I refer to this as the humanistic baseline for the concept of education.

FROM THE HUMANISTIC BASELINE TO FOUR BASIC NEEDS

The next sort of question we have to ask is this: If any given system of education—regardless of the social goals toward which it is directed—must meet a humanistic baseline in order to count as a system of specifically *education*, then how do we determine what is involved in meeting that humanistic baseline? What sort of education activates latent potential for general human flourishing? This is also to ask which account of human flourishing we should use to give content to the humanistic baseline for education. As we pursue an answer to this question, we will also have to ask whether it is possible to have an approach to education that integrates the two perspectives provided by its system-level and its microlevel justifications. A coherent account of the purposes of education surely requires such an integration or alignment.

As we initiate our hunt for an acceptable eudaemonistic account of the nature of education, we can define the stakes of the search by reaching back again, if briefly, to the first theorist of education in the Western tradition. In Athens of the fourth century BCE, in his dialogue, *The Republic*, the ancient Greek philosopher Plato argued that the differences among people are such that each should be educated to perform excellently the one kind of work at which she will excel. This would make us all virtuous and therefore happy, he argued, as would assuming our places in a highly stratified society in which adults perform the specific roles assigned to each (for instance, political leadership, military service, craftsmanship, trading, or agriculture). But this is not a democratic answer to the question, forced upon us by the logic of practices, of how to justify not merely the institutions of education but also the actions undertaken while educating. And just as Plato's answer is antidemocratic, so too is it illiberal, even if only *avant la lettre*. Liberalism depends on the idea that the ends of the state and of the individual are separable to a meaningful degree. Plato, of course, argued the opposite view that city and soul cannot ultimately adopt divergent aims.[33] He achieved an integration of the system-level and action-specific justifications for education by proposing a form of education whose purpose was to fit each individual to his assigned social role.

Against Plato, a democratic answer to the question of the kind of education that would achieve full human flourishing starts from a different view of human nature—namely, that despite the differences among us, we are all capable of doing multiple jobs, at the very least those of performing our own particular excellence and also of acting politically as citizens.[34] To flesh out a democratic account of full human flourishing, we would profit, I think, from turning now to the work of another mid-twentieth-century philosopher not often considered in concert with Rawls. The person I have in mind is Hannah Arendt, a German-Jewish émigrée who came to the United States in 1941. Her 1958 book *The Human Condition* is driven by a consideration of the issue of well-being from the perspective of the individual instead of the social whole. Given the historical proximity of Rawls's 1955 article and Arendt's 1958 book, it is perhaps unsurprising that there should be resonances among them. More surprising is that the lines of thought in contemporary political philosophy that flow from each rush on so separately from one another. Interestingly, Arendt's *The Human Condition* provides a valuably democratic account of human flourishing that can serve as a foundation for integrating our two concepts of education: our macrolevel social utilitarian concept and our microlevel eudaemonistic concept.

In *The Human Condition*, Arendt famously expounds on the content and import of three core human activities: labor, work, and action. Labor is that which we undertake out of biological necessity—that which we do, in other words, to feed ourselves. It also encompasses sexual reproduction and the energies devoted to child-rearing. Work is that which we do out of creative effort, to build the things—whether physical or cultural—that shape our world and establish our social connections with others. Labor and work overlap with each other, since our romantic relationships are products of our social art and, of course, create the context within which we may also pursue biological reproduction. Finally, action identifies the effort we make together as political creatures, struggling in conditions of pluralistic diversity to come to collective decisions about our polity's course of action.[35]

Arendt's arguments about labor, work, and action have garnered significant scholarly attention, yet one important detail has been overlooked. By describing work, labor, and action as typifying every human existence, Arendt sought to reverse centuries, even millennia, of philosophical effort to differentiate social roles with reference to these activities.[36] Earlier philosophers had assigned to a different social class each of the three domains of activity that for Arendt defined the human condition of each individual. In the idealized Greek city of Aristotle, for instance, slaves were tasked with securing a stable economic base for life, tradesmen were tasked with contributing to the realm of creativity, and citizens were tasked with participating in politics. Similarly, Plato assigned these tasks to farmers, traders, craftsmen, soldiers, and political leaders and expected very little mobility among these groups.

With her incandescent and liberatory philosophical imagination, Arendt de-differentiated these three roles and recombined them into an account of the experience of every individual—themselves the marks of the human condition for each one of us. On an Arendtian account, the potential of the modern union of economics and politics is that we can build polities that are nonstratified such that each individual is responsible for securing his own subsistence (rather than exploiting others[37]), has a life scope that makes it possible to create meaningful social worlds (both intimate and communal), and has a platform for participating in politics. Individual human flourishing, then, depends on the activation of a potential that inheres in all human beings—as a feature of the human condition—to succeed at labor, work, and political action simultaneously.

On the basis of Arendt's arguments in *The Human Condition*, then, we can identify four basic human potentialities that should be activated by education. (I am splitting the potentiality captured by "labor" into two.) Through education, we need to do the following:

1. Prepare ourselves for breadwinning work (labor, part 1)
2. Prepare ourselves for civic and political engagement (action)
3. Prepare ourselves for creative self-expression and world making (work)
4. Prepare ourselves for rewarding relationships in spaces of intimacy and leisure (labor, part 2, overlapping with work)

We recognize that the capacities relevant to all these domains are flourishing when we see young people become adults who can support themselves economically without exploiting others; take their place among a world of adult creators, including as creators of rewarding intimate relationships; and participate effectively in their polity's political life. When the humanistic baseline for the microlevel concept of education is given content from such democratic eudaemonism, it orients us toward a pedagogic practice that is in itself egalitarian in that it seeks to meet the same range of needs for all students. Yet there is also another way in which this conceptualization of education makes a contribution to egalitarianism.

When one takes a look at this list of basic educational needs generated from Arendt's democratic eudaemonism, one quickly notices that the utilitarian social justifications for a system of education—that a polity as a whole secures economic competitiveness and, in the case of a democracy, an engaged and effective citizenry—align with two of the four needs any individual must meet with education. Each person's individual need to prepare for breadwinning work and for civic and political engagement is simply the other side of the coin of the social need for broad economic competitiveness and an engaged citizenry. In other words, public goods and private goods come together here, and analyzing education in terms of an opposition between them is not necessarily helpful. Similarly, the state's "utilitarian" goods (economic competitiveness and a flourishing citizenry) turn out to be features of an individual's eudaemonistic good if merely considered from a different perspective. Although a state seeks an economically successful population, each individual flourishes only when his potential for successful labor is appropriately activated. And although a democracy needs an engaged and effective citizenry, each individual flourishes only when his potential for action is appropriately tapped.

When we see how the social and the individual come together, bringing the two concepts of education into alignment with each other, we also learn something important about our own contemporary conversations about education. Our current conversations emphasize only one of the social justifications for education—namely, the economic—leaving the state's need to cultivate effective citizens largely to the side. I'll return to that topic in chapter 2, for that is where the truly egalitarian work of this humanistic concept of education comes into play.

Yet for all the surprising proximity, then, between the system-level goals of education and the individual-level goals that emerge from the eudaemonistic account, we should also be grateful that the alignment between social goals and our individual goals is only partial. It should be a cause of relief that two of the basic needs defining the humanistic baseline for the practice of education—for creative self-expression and world making and for rewarding relationships in spaces of intimacy and leisure—do not align with the system-level justifications for education. We don't want the state to colonize our social lives as creatures who build our worlds with others through creative self-expression and who pursue rewarding relationships in spaces of intimacy and leisure.

Yet while we do not wish the state to colonize those spaces, we do need to ensure that the state leaves space for them. That is, if in failing to see those spaces, the state begins to override them, then that is simply another form of colonization. And this brings us to the topic of just how the humanistic baseline for education might point us toward a reorientation of our education policy discussions generally.

Rawls helped us see that we must consider the goals of educational systems, on the one hand, and of teachers with specific students, on the other. Arendt offers us a eudaemonism that permits bringing social and individual goods into alignment with one another on a democratic footing. Thinking clearly about education requires shifting effectively back and forth between these two registers: the social and the individual, categories that track neither a public good versus private good distinction nor a simplistic utilitarian versus nonutilitarian distinction. If the state is to support a system of education that remains a system of *education* as distinct from some other practice, it needs to leave institutions the room to educate such that their pedagogic practices meet the requirements of the humanistic baseline.

THE HUMANISTIC BASELINE AND EDUCATION POLICY

This idea of two concepts of education should affect reflection on educational policy by requiring us to consider any given policy proposal through each of two lenses. We can assess a policy for its success in meeting the social goods we have in view—perhaps global economic competitiveness. But we also need to assess the policy by asking whether the actions it requires and institutions it establishes also satisfy the humanistic baseline that justifies actual educating.

Let me illustrate this point, very briefly, with a few schematic remarks about the policy topic of accountability. Once one sees that there are in fact two kinds of justifications relevant to thinking about education, one realizes that there must also be two kinds of accountability relevant to the practice. The system of education, as a whole, needs to be assessed in relation to the utilitarian justification, which justified drawing the social practice of education within the political realm in the first place. But individual and particular instances of teaching need to be assessed in relation to the eudaemonistic justification that should properly structure the relationship between teacher and student.

Does our present approach to accountability employ this distinction? It does not. We wish to hold the system as a whole accountable for the production of economically competitive citizens, but to do so, we test individual children not for each child's own sake but in order to track change over time in the performance of student cohorts.[38] Individual students are, in other words, made the instruments for judging something other than themselves and their own flourishing.[39] How might we otherwise approach accountability?

We wish to know three things in the context of K–12 education: how whole schools are doing, how individual teachers are doing, and how specific students are doing. We might think of the first question as requiring system-level practices of accountability and the latter two as requiring practices of accountability that pertain to the microlevel of the teacher-student relationship and student learning. Remember the old teacher joke:

Question: "What do you teach?"
Answer: "Students."

Teachers should indeed be held accountable, but for the flourishing (or failure to flourish) of individual children along all the dimensions identified in the democratic eudaemonistic justification for education—progress toward economic self-sufficiency, progress toward a capacity for social and cultural creation, and progress toward a capacity to participate in political life.

System-level practices of accountability should be constructed out of measures that can capture system-wide effects without interfering with the individual teacher-student relationship. We need measurements that touch the system as such, not the particular moves or actions made within it. But then we also need visibility into the quality of particular instances of teaching. Finally, in order to make continuous improvement possible, we need to understand the chains of connection between what happens at the micro-level and system-level outcomes. The trick to accountability is to use appropriate system-level measures, to employ appropriate approaches to evaluation of teaching and assessment of learning at the microlevel, and to establish connections between these two types of evaluation in order to support rigorous but fair accountability practices and continuous improvement in the practices of specific teachers and functioning of specific schools. The challenges of doing this are enormous, although not, I think, insurmountable. If we start with the first question—regarding the appropriate system-level measures—and walk through the other questions thereafter, we ought to be able to step delicately and carefully toward a useful framework for thinking about accountability.

First, we should begin by noting that system-level measures of school performance that touch the system without interfering with the particular moves made within the system are available. Imaginative educational reformers have already identified some that are now commonly part of the conversation. Thus Larry Rosenstock of High-Tech High in San Diego, California, proposes that we track the following:

1. Of the entering ninth graders in that education entity (school, district, or state), what percentage graduated from a four-year college?
2. Of those students who qualify for free and reduced lunch of those ninth grade entrants, what percentage graduated from a four-year college?

3. Of those ninth graders not in poverty, what percentage graduated from a four-year college?

4. Finally, what relative mixtures/concentrations of answers to questions 2 and 3 were most efficacious for getting the students represented in answer number 2 through college?[40]

These four questions are to be treated as a bundle. Only by asking them together can we gauge how well schools are doing at counteracting the impact of poverty on educational outcomes.

Importantly, indicators such as these are of little immediate use in helping schools improve.[41] The data points to which Rosenstock draws our attention are what are called "lagging indicators." The results show up several years after the performance for which they're supposed to provide a basis for evaluation and accountability. College completion, for instance, is generally measured in terms of how many students complete their course of studies within six years—by that time, the principal of the sending school will, in all likelihood, have moved on, and the school's faculty will have changed. The longer the temporal gap between the intervention and the measured outcome, the less useful the measured outcome is for accountability purposes. Lagging indicators therefore need to be correlated to "leading indicators" if they are to be of any use for efforts to evaluate and improve school performance.

In contrast to lagging indicators, "leading indicators" are predictive. They identify particular features of school and teacher performance in the present that correlate with the future outcomes of interest—that is, the lagging indicators. Principals and teachers can manage around those leading indicators in the expectation that time will bear them out, with positive results appearing in the lagging indicators down the road. In fact, student testing is supposed to serve as just such a leading indicator, although as researchers have shown, student testing is more strongly predictive of future test scores than of things like whether students struggle or succeed with high school course work or complete college.[42] We therefore want leading indicators that do a better job than test scores of predicting attainment outcomes like college completion while minimizing interference with or negative effects on instructional practice.

It is in fact possible to develop leading indicators that, like the lagging outcome indicators, do not interfere with the actual practice of teaching and learning. Researchers at the University of Chicago Consortium for Chicago School Research (CCSR) have done so, developing an extensive set of leading indicators to guide the work done by schools and teachers in fostering academic achievement. These indicators are developed on the basis of measures that perform better than standardized tests in predicting student attainment. They also make use of readily available data already independently generated by the practice of educating, so using these data does not interfere with educating. One such indicator is the on-track status of ninth graders in a given school (with respect to attendance, grades, and course pass rates); on-track status is a better predictor of high school graduation than eighth-grade test scores or socioeconomic status. Moreover, identification of this first indicator allows for the development of others. Since "schools that cultivate strong student-teacher relationships, make high school relevant for students, and engage their students average fewer failures, better grades, and better attendance," the consortium has developed indicators to help schools judge how well they are doing these foundational things.[43] These reformers are confident that that they can judge which schools are succeeding and which are not with rubrics and metrics that track systemic effects without interfering with the activity of teaching to do so. Measures of system-level performance are most valuable when they are, as in this case, organically linked (as test scores are not) to specific features of the activity of teaching. In addition to supporting continuous improvement, such indicators give parents and students much more powerful tools than test scores for holding schools accountable, because they give parents and students actionable policies and improvements to propose instead of the generic demand that schools "raise scores."[44]

In another example of an approach to assessment and accountability that seeks to lessen the negative impacts on instructional practice of test-based accountability, the innovative Local Control Accountability Program in California uses "indicators like students' access to strong college and career-going curriculum, parent involvement, graduation rates, attendance, and school climate," alongside state testing results generated solely for the purpose of assessment.[45] Importantly, this program also takes advantage of another underutilized resource: assessment data generated by instructional practice itself—in this case, advanced placement (AP) test results. The College Board develops its exams in close collaboration with instructors and

AP curricula developers. In addition, AP instructors serve as graders for the exams. In other words, AP exams function very similarly, at scale, to how any given individual teacher uses exams in the classroom: a good teacher builds a curriculum and, as part of that work, develops formative (or midstream) and summative (or final) assessments to check whether students' work meets the objectives. The exams are in fact part of the instructional practice. Indeed, the craft of teaching has always depended on forms of assessment as *part of the practice itself.*

Grades are another example of the integration of assessment in the practice of teachers. They are very good predictors of students' long-term success. They do, however, also correlate with nonacademic features of the student-teacher relationship, and this is clearly problematic.[46] In other words, grades currently serve as only imperfect assessment measures of student learning. Yet we need not abandon them as a resource. We should instead focus on improving their use by teachers. Precisely because teaching is a craft, with its own internal standards of excellence, the practice of teaching itself generates a vast store of data that can be used to assess students and evaluate teachers without interfering with the practice of teaching. Teachers are constantly assessing their students—with exams, written assignments, projects, and the like. The archive of materials generated by instructional practice already provides a remarkable treasure trove of data for seeing what and how students are learning and how teachers are performing. The challenge is to learn how to make use of all this already existing data to assess student achievement, evaluate teachers, and support continuous improvement. To do these things, we would need to gather data from assessment practices that are *part of* the craft of teaching itself, make what are often tacit internal standards of excellence explicit, validate the value of those standards through research, evaluate the gathered data against those internal standards, and use those evaluations to work on improving teachers' craft.[47] The goal, in the words of one set of educational researchers, is to tap into the "mutual responsibility educators have to one another to live up to the quality standards of their profession."[48] But this goal advances the conversation about accountability only if those quality standards have been made explicit and tested by researchers for their validity.

The final question, then, in thinking through a framework for assessment and accountability that connects system-level indicators to indicators that emerge from instructional practice itself, is how to support principals and teachers in working with the latter set of indicators to manage toward the former set. The challenge here is that any indicator becomes less valuable once it is used for high-stakes purposes in the context of a purely numerical evaluation. Numerical results can be massaged through all sorts of practices that don't directly relate to good teaching, like controlling student enrollments in order to improve a school's test scores. Consequently, the practices for using these indicators to assess teaching and school performance should be constructed such that their incentivizing power incentivizes what we want—namely, better teaching, not cheating or gaming the system.

To my eye (and that of many others as well), the Professional Growth System in Montgomery County, Maryland, and in particular its use of a "peer assistance and review" (PAR) process to mentor new and underperforming teachers, meets all the criteria I've laid out in this section for identifying a strong approach to accountability. Let me first explain how PAR works, and then I'll say a few words about how it meets my criteria.

New teachers and teachers identified by their principals as underperforming are referred to the PAR process.[49] Over the course of a year, twenty-four consulting teachers, master teachers who have agreed to step out of the classroom for three years, work with the PAR cohort and provide supports, including the following:

- Informal and formal observations
- Written and verbal standards-based feedback
- Equitable classroom practice
- Coaching sessions
- Lesson planning
- Model lessons
- Coteaching modeling
- Peer observations
- Classroom management
- Time management
- Alignment of school support

Over the course of the year, the consulting teachers "document their work but do not do formal evaluations"; they merely judge whether the teachers meet the standards.[50] The dossier of their documentation is then turned over to a review panel consisting of eight teachers and eight principals. That panel considers each candidate for nonrenewal/dismissal, an additional year of PAR, or release into the regular evaluation process that covers all staff members (and focuses on modes of assessment that build on, rather than interrupt, instructional practice). The program was initiated in 2000, and between then and 2011, approximately five hundred teachers were removed from the classroom. This is "in a system of about 150,000 students with approximately 11,000 teachers and 200 schools. Over the same period, nearly 5,000 teachers . . . successfully completed the PAR process."[51]

What about the system-level outcomes of the PAR approach to accountability? Here is how educational researcher Stan Karp presents those using the data we presently have available: "Over the past decade, student achievement as measured by Maryland's state assessments has increased across-the-board in every student subgroup—by race, ethnicity, and income level. Achievement gaps have narrowed at all grade levels in both math and reading. In grades 3 and 5 math, and grade 7 reading, the gap narrowed by 16 points; in grades 3 and 5 reading, it narrowed by more than 20 points. Beyond the test scores, 84 percent of Montgomery County's students go on to college and 63 percent earn degrees."[52] In 2011, journalist Michael Winerip indicated that "2.5 percent of all black children in America who pass an Advanced Placement test live in Montgomery County, more than five times its share of the nation's black population."[53] Neither of these batches of measures—those using state assessment test results and the data on college completion and AP—is of the sort that we want. The testing regime, of course, interrupts the instructional practice. The data on college completion and AP test scores do not tell us enough without separating out the data, as Rosenstock suggests, for students not in poverty and those on the free and reduced lunch program. Without separating the system-level data in that way, we cannot see the degree to which the schools themselves make an impact that goes beyond the effects on student performance of parental education and family social economic status. Many governmental and civil service officials reside in Montgomery County; for this reason, the county's student populations probably have above-average representations of African American students with parents with high levels of education. We can improve these measures.

In place of test scores, we might explore the use of grades, which emerge out of instructional practice, to evaluate reductions in achievement gaps; the college completion data also need refinement to a more sophisticated level.

The PAR teacher evaluation and accountability system, then, connects long-term system-level outcomes—college completion, for instance—to leading indicators (here the imperfect ones of state assessment scores but also AP test scores) and tracks teacher impact on student learning in terms of features that define excellence at the craft of teaching, like lesson planning and classroom management. Here we see a merger of system-level modes of evaluation for accountability with microlevel practices of student assessment, teacher evaluation, and teacher accountability. This captures the sort of balance we should pursue, I think.

Policy alternatives, then, rest on answers to deeper questions posed by the logic of education as a practice. They carry with them implicit answers to the question of how we justify both a system of education and also the practice of actually teaching. By forcing to the surface our thinking about the two concepts of education—the state-level and the microlevel concepts—I hope to have provided a framework to support more rigorous analysis of our policy options. By arguing for the importance of a humanistic baseline in thinking about what education is, I also hope to have restored some balance to our policy conversations, which tend to turn around the state-level concept of education. Most important, when we shift our gaze from the social to the individual justification of education and orient ourselves to the humanistic baseline, democratically defined, we are restoring the egalitarian potential of education in itself. The humanistic baseline requires that we think about the education of all students in the context of a broad notion of flourishing. Thus the humanistic baseline reinforces an egalitarian orientation toward human dignity that can disappear if we focus exclusively on the state-level justifications of education, which instrumentalize the student.

In chapter 2, I will turn to the topic of civic education or, to use more Arendtian language, preparation for participatory readiness. This is the policy domain in which the intrinsic egalitarian potential of education most fully shows itself.

CHAPTER 2

] Participatory Readiness

λόγος δυνάστης μέγας ἐστίν, ὃς σμικροτάτωι σώματι καὶ
ἀφανεστάτωι θειότατα ἔργα ἀποτελεῖ·
Speech is a great power, which achieves the most divine works
by means of the smallest and least visible body.
—Gorgias, "Encomium to Helen"

INTRODUCING PARTICIPATORY READINESS

Let me reprise briefly. Our conversations about education are often muddled
because we fail to distinguish between two concepts of education: one that
justifies the practice at a societal level and the other that justifies actual instances of particular teachers teaching particular students. When we focus
on the latter, we see the importance of fulfilling four basic human needs:
breadwinning, civic and political engagement, creative self-expression and
world making, and rewarding relationships in spaces of intimacy and leisure.
Yet clarifying these needs also highlights that our public discourse about education, our articulations of our collective goals, routinely leave out the civic.
We have seen that, for instance, according to the Common Core State Standards, education "must ensure **all** American students are prepared for the
global economic workplace" (emphasis in original).[1] In general, the rhetoric
of educational policy relies almost exclusively on advocating the goals of college and career readiness. This is true despite the fact that civic experience is
important to both concepts of education—the social and the individual. The
civic has, in short, gone AWOL. In this chapter, I will rectify this by developing an account of education for "participatory readiness."

What exactly is "participatory readiness"? First, the idea of being prepared
to participate captures prospects of participation at several social levels: not
only that of the political community but also that of intimate and commu-
nitarian relationships. Think again of the four needs I derived from Arendt.
Our flourishing as creators entails our engagement in cultural communities
of meaning, and even our success in the realm of labor requires participation
in social relationships. "Participatory readiness" defines our preparation for
civic and political life, but it also undergirds our preparation in all the areas
in which we hope to prosper. When young people leave school or college, we

hope that they are prepared to participate effectively at work, in communities, and in love. One might well want to pause on the question of what "participatory readiness" entails at the intimate or social level—particularly given the contemporary crisis around sexual assault on college campuses. But the question of what it means to participate well in civic and political life also deserves our fulsome attention. The reason to prioritize this topic—despite the urgencies of the social pathologies of our campuses—is its centrality to our political pathology, the intertwining problems of political and economic inequality.

Before I turn to the components of "participatory readiness," then, and what we know about the kinds of education that can achieve them, I'd like to take a moment to expand on just how civic and political agency and their cultivation are relevant to our understanding of equality and any effort to address issues of inequality, however those are specified.

PARTICIPATORY READINESS AND EQUALITY

The first link between a broad education for "participatory readiness" and equality is obvious. The idea that all students should be educated for political participation—and not merely a select few prepared for political leadership as suggested in Plato—is already an egalitarian feature of the humanistic baseline education, as I've defined that. In seeking to give content to the humanistic baseline for education, I described myself as employing a democratic eudaemonism developed from Arendt. My embrace of democracy imported an ideal of political equality to the core idea of human flourishing that education supports. In other words, I follow Hannah Arendt (and others) in seeing a basic human need to participate in the realm of action as explaining why, among possible regime types, democracy is not only desirable but also the most just.[2] Given that, according to this argument, political participation is necessary for a flourishing life and given that education is preparation for a flourishing life, our curricula and pedagogies must prepare people for an Arendtian life of action. The goal is to maximize participation and thereby come closer to realizing an ideal of political equality, while also providing the specific sense of fulfillment that accrues to each individual through the experience of empowerment. This version of the microlevel concept of education, one based in *democratic* eudaemonism, foregrounds an aspiration to prepare students to participate in their communities and polities, an aspiration that flows from and then, in turn, reinforces a commitment to political equality.

The egalitarian significance of this preparation of the young for civic and political life extends, however, beyond politics. It stretches to every domain for which it matters who makes the decisions that define our collective lives. The importance of "participatory readiness" therefore touches even the realm of economics. Here we can return to the many scholars who propose education as the main remedy to income and wealth inequality. They do so accurately but miss one of the reasons to make that recommendation.

Most arguments that education is the solution to economic inequality stress education's potential to disseminate skills broadly within a population. Such broad dissemination is expected to drive down the wage premium on expertise and help compress the income distribution. I am thinking again of Thomas Piketty's arguments but also of the work of Claudia Goldin and Larry Katz. On this line of thought, education is presumed to bring with it positional advantage. That is, those who have more education — more skills — can be presumed to reap more market rewards than those with lesser educational attainment. Narrowing gaps in educational attainment across the population, or equalizing the distribution of educational goods, should, then, also reduce the positional advantage that accrues to education and reduce, for instance, income inequality. Political philosopher Rob Reich, coeditor with me of the volume *Education, Justice, and Equality*, has drawn my attention to the work of the economist Fred Hirsch on the idea of positionality. Hirsch quips, "If everyone stands on tiptoe, no one sees any better."[3] We might also say, "If everyone stands on tiptoe, then no one is too seriously overshadowed."

But there are limits to how much the positional advantage of education can be moderated through the dissemination of technological skills. To see this more clearly, it will be helpful to focus again on how economist Thomas Piketty treats the relationship between education and equality. To reprise, early in *Capital*, he writes the following: "Historical experience suggests that the principal mechanism for convergence [of incomes and wealth] at the international as well as the domestic level is the diffusion of knowledge. In other words, the poor catch up with the rich to the extent that they achieve the same level of technological know-how, skill, and education."[4]

Yet when he turns to policy prescription in part 4 of the book, his treatment of education is relatively brief and mainly forms a part of his discussion of the modernization of the social state.[5] By this, he means that "the tax and transfer systems that are the heart of the modern social state are in constant need of reform and modernization, because they have achieved a level of complexity that makes them difficult to understand and threatens to undermine their social and economic efficacy."[6] Given the emphasis Piketty places on education as a force for equality in the opening section of the book, the brevity of the final discussion disappoints.

Piketty's recommendations for educational policy are quite spare. They are also familiar: egalitarian-minded reformers ought to work toward the broadest possible accessibility of educational institutions to the population; elite institutions, which currently serve mainly privileged youth from the highest income brackets, need to broaden the backgrounds from which they draw their students; states should increase investment in "high-quality professional training and advanced educational opportunities and allow broader segments of the population to have access to them"[7]; and schools should be run efficiently.

In conditions of growth, the increasing accessibility of education serves to reduce income inequality, and eventually wealth, only if it shifts how types of degrees are distributed across the population. That is, the spread of education has little impact on inequality if everyone who once had a high school degree now earns a college degree and all those who previously secured only an eighth-grade level of education now attain the high school credential. Instead, one needs to shift those in lower educational bands into higher bands, without concomitant upward positional moves of those in the higher bands.

As I have indicated, these policy proposals closely track those of Claudia Goldin and Larry Katz in *The Race between Education and Technology*.[8] In their argument, rising income inequality in the United States can be explained to a significant degree by the wage premium on skill. As technological innovations emerge and generate a demand for new skills that are undersupplied, those in possession of the skills in demand will reap rewards in the form of higher income. In order for a society to see egalitarian income distributions, on their argument, education must race to maintain democratized skill provision that keeps up with the changing demands of an economy fueled by technological development.

Yet, as Piketty points out, the wage premium on skill can explain only a part of the growth in income inequality in the United States. The growth at

the highest end, in the incomes accruing to "supermanagers," in his vocabulary, reflects social norms that have coalesced around the acceptability of
sky-high executive pay. In his argument, these social norms have coalesced
as part of the growth of political ideology that endorses untrammeled meri-
tocracy. Supercharged salaries are held up, rhetorically, as evidence of a sup-
posedly fair and equally supercharged operation of talent.

The question, then, of how to temper income inequality on Piketty's argument has to do not only with the dissemination of skill but also with social
norms and how those can be changed. Here is where he misses one of education's most egalitarian impacts. In an important 2006 paper titled "Why
Does Democracy Need Education?," economists Edward L. Glaeser, Giacomo Ponzetto, and Andrei Shleifer identify a correlation between education and democracy that they argue has causal force, with education caus-
ing democracy.[9] They point to a more fundamental relationship or, in their
words, "primitive connection," between education and participation and test
three hypotheses for why education might cause participation. Perhaps it
does so through the provision of indoctrination; perhaps through the provision of interpersonal skills (through reading and writing and the provision of
"soft skills"); or perhaps through a general increase in the personal material
benefits of participation. They rule out the first and third hypotheses and
make the case that education causes participation because it makes people
ready to participate.

And what flows from participation? Very often, but not always, it is democratic contestation. (The purpose of the qualification is to acknowledge, as
Glaeser, Ponzetto, and Shleifer point out, that the rise of European Fascism
also drew on the energies of students.) As scholars of the US civil rights movement like Charles Payne and social movement scholars like Cathy Cohen and
Deva Woodley have shown, political contestation can drive change in social
norms.[10] This is where education's true egalitarian potential comes into play.
It supplies the basis for forms of participatory democracy that might contest
the labor market rules that deliver insupportable forms of income inequality.

Piketty's failure to make this point is surprising. In a 2015 paper titled
"The Rise and Decline of General Laws of Capitalism," the economist Daron
Acemoglu and political scientist Jim Robinson have pointed out that arguments like those of Katz and Goldin presume a stable framework of technology and political institutions.[11] They put this point as a critique of Piketty,

arguing that his account of a future where rates of return on capital will consistently outstrip income accruing to labor fails because, in their view, it ignores politics: "The quest for general laws of capitalism, or any economic system, is misguided because it is a-institutional. It ignores that it is the institutions and the political equilibrium of a society that determine how technology evolves, how markets function, and how the gains from various different economic arrangements are distributed."[12] As examples of the impact of popular participation on the economy, Acemoglu and Robinson highlight late nineteenth- and early twentieth-century Populist and then Progressive mobilizations in the United States that led to reductions of corporate power—a turn of events that refuted one of Marx's general laws, they argue.

But their argument is not fair to Piketty, who does repeatedly underscore that policy frameworks, institutional choices, and social norms affect how income and wealth will be distributed. Thus, he writes, "In order to understand the dynamics of wage inequality, we must introduce other factors, such as the institutions and rules that govern the operation of the labor market in each society."[13] In other words, Piketty fully understands the importance of politics to his picture of the economy. The point he misses is to underscore the relationship between education and equality that rests on the link between education and preparation for participation.

The preparation of citizens through education for civic and political engagement supports the pursuit of political equality, but political equality, in turn, may well engender more egalitarian approaches to the economy. An education that prepares students for civic and political engagement brings into play the prospect of political contestation around issues of economic fairness. In other words, education can affect income inequality not merely by spreading technical skills and compressing the income distribution. It can even have an effect on income inequality by increasing a society's political competitiveness and thereby impacting "how technology evolves, how markets function, and how the gains from various different economic arrangements are distributed."[14]

The idea of "participatory readiness" and the concept of equality, in short, have several linkages. An education that prepares students for civic and political engagement brings not only a concept of political equality into play but also the prospect of political contestation around issues of economic fairness. Insofar as technology frameworks and political institutions are malleable, the status of education as a positional good may itself be susceptible to change, and the degree of its positionality will in all likelihood vary with the political context. If an education for participatory readiness can affect a society's level of political competitiveness, it may also drive changes not only in the distribution of education but even in its positionality.[15] Consequently, the most effective way for us to direct our educational system toward egalitarian ends could well be to focus on participatory readiness.

When we think about equality in the context of education, we tend to think above all about distributional questions. We imagine that we will have an egalitarian system when we've managed to fund a system that will genuinely offer the possibility of an equal level of attainment (as distinguished from achievement[16]) to all (or nearly all) students. But we may need to move the conversation one step back and remind ourselves that fair economic outcomes may themselves depend on genuine political equality. If this is right, then an education focused on participatory readiness, and not merely technical skill, better helps us understand the linkage between pedagogy and equality.

But if "participatory readiness" is so important, just what should students get ready for? And how do we expect them to participate?

PARTICIPATORY READINESS: READY FOR WHAT?

A basic challenge when answering the question of what students should get ready for is reflected in a certain instability in our common vocabulary. Would we like to say that we should prepare them for civic engagement? Or for political participation? In regard to this question, we are confused.[17] Thus far in my argument, I have repeatedly used the pleonastic phrase "civic and political life," and this reflects what I take to be a broadly shared confusion. After all, don't those two words mean fundamentally the same thing? Their etymological roots are similar: "political" and "civic" come respectively from the Greek and Latin terms for "city." Why, then, use both at once? These terms have come to have two distinct rhetorical valences. "Civic" is a safe word. It suggests public action undertaken through approved venues and within the confines of long-standing public agendas. "Political" is a more charged term. It invokes approved actions such as voting and holding office, but it also suggests protest action, activism, and advocacy—all of which make us nervous when we come to discussions of things like curriculum and pedagogy. We don't, for instance, commonly think that a K–12 education or college education should be organized around teaching people Saul Alinsky's *Rules for Radicals*.[18] Yet Alinsky's text does instill participatory readiness of at least *some kind or another*. And whatever kind it is, we are most likely to call an education in Alinsky "political," rather than "civic."

The strange uncertainty around the definition of "political" struck me with a special force when I had the occasion to watch the video of a recent panel that gathered together three young leaders of digital associations. These young people were respectively engaged in activities like supporting marriage equality, disseminating Hayekian economic ideas, and claiming space in the public sphere for American Muslims. When asked whether they thought of themselves as political, each said "no."[19] This fact underscores the challenge of trying to define the content of an education for "participatory readiness." We can't quite bring ourselves to agree on whether our object is the "civic" or the "political," and this is partly because we no longer esteem the "political." The lack of equilibrium in our vocabulary—do we want to talk about the "civic" or do we want to talk about the "political"—reflects the current absence of any single, unified conception of what it means to participate in public life.

A historical view can bring perspective to the situation in which we find ourselves with regard to our conceptions of citizenship. The sociologist and communications scholar Michael Schudson has made the important point that models of civic education in any given time and place tend to track that time's reigning ideology about citizenship.[20] In the case of the United States, he identifies four separate models of civic agency that have emerged since the founding—with each model stemming from the period's reigning ideals and generating a distinctive approach to socializing the young for political participation.

In the young republic, politics was dominated, Schudson argues, by a model of the citizen as the "trusted, solid" individual—a (white, male) property owner whose central activity was to vote for esteemed leaders whose wise hands would set the community's course. A religious education directed toward matters of character predominated. With the rise of populist politics and mass political parties, the citizen evolved into the "party loyalist"—an individual who turned out for party parades and events, voted for the slate, and reaped economic benefits like employment opportunities through party membership. The intellectual demands were minimal; to vote a party ticket, not even literacy was necessary. With the rise of the progressive era and the professionalization of political administration and journalism, the country saw the emergence of "the informed voter" as the model for citizenship. Voting was still the citizen's main activity, but that citizen was supposed to enter the now private ballot box having consumed high quality information provided by journalists. With the civil rights era came the "rights-conscious" citizen; individuals needed to be both more self-aware about their own rights and more attentive to those of others. The citizen's tool kit now included the courtroom and tactics like public litigation.

I think it's currently impossible to find a single, unifying model of citizenship dominating our culture—and our uncertainty about the terms "civic" and "political" is just one symptom of this difficulty.[21] Nonetheless, we can identify a handful of models currently bumping and jostling each other in our collective imagination. To spot them, though, we will need to establish as a backdrop a broad, philosophical conceptualization of the range of action types that can characterize public life, so that we can consider which features of that range currently have the greatest salience. Just as Hannah Arendt's philosophical views were helpful in identifying the humanistic baseline, her work can advance our thinking here, too. We can draw on her account of *action* to limn the backdrop against which to assess just how, in practice, we seem to conceive of the political life these days.

In Arendt's account of action, citizenship is the activity of cocreating a way of life; it is the activity of world building. The concept, fully understood, extends beyond legal categories of membership in political units. The activity of citizenship—of cocreation and world building—can occur at many different social levels: in a neighborhood or school; in a networked community or association; in a city, state, or nation; at a global level. In my own work, I further specify this idea of civic agency as multifaceted and involving three core tasks.[22] First, there is disinterested deliberation around a public problem.[23] Here, the model is the Athenian citizens gathered in the assembly, or the town halls of colonial New Hampshire, or public representatives behaving reasonably in the halls of a legislature. Second, there is prophetic work to shift a society's codes of values; in the public opinion and communications literature, this is now called "frame shifting."[24] Think here of the rhetorical power of the nineteenth-century abolitionist Harriet Beecher

Stowe and civil rights leader Martin Luther King Jr. Finally, there is transparently and passionately interested "fair fighting," where a given public actor adopts a cause and pursues it passionately, never pretending to disinterestedness.[25] One might think of the nineteenth-century activists for women's rights, Elizabeth Cady Stanton, Susan B. Anthony, and Matilda Joslyn Gage.

The ideal civic agent combines capacities to carry out all three of these tasks ethically and justly. Let's take the nineteenth-century women's rights activist Elizabeth Stanton Cady as an example. At the Seneca Falls Convention, she had to function in a deliberative mode for the debate about the text of the Declaration of Sentiments, but when she drafted that text, before the convention's deliberations, she functioned in the prophetic mode, as in her many speeches. Finally, in campaigning for legal change, as in the adoption of the Married Woman's Property Act in New York and similar laws in other states, she functioned as an activist.

Yet if these—deliberation, prophesy, and contestation—are the rudimentary components of civic agency, they do not in themselves determine the content of any given historical moment's conception of citizenship. There is no need for each of these functions to be combined in a single role or citizenly persona, nor is there any guarantee that all three will operate in each historical context. Diverse regime types—from the authoritarian to the liberal to the tribal—have been known to try to shut down heterodox prophets. One or another of these roles may be foregrounded, and it is altogether possible for these tasks to become separated from one another, generating distinguishable kinds of civic roles. I think this latter situation obtains today.

Distinct, alternative roles and personae have developed that emphasize one or another of these three core tasks of civic agency or some combination of them. I designate these roles as the "civically engaged individual"; the "activist," or "political entrepreneur"; and the "professional politician." Following Schudson's example, we can distinguish these roles by how they define the tasks of civic agency, how they connect to the levers of power, and how they place intellectual and psychological demands on their practitioners.[26]

The "civically engaged individual" focuses on the task of disinterested deliberation and actions that can be said to flow from it. Such citizens focus on pursuing "universal" values, "disinterestedness," "critical thinking," and "bipartisan" projects[27]—hence our use of the safe word "civic" for this category of civic agency. Next come the activist and the politician. They are "political" actors, and the unsafe and sometimes unsavory nature of the activity conducted through these second two roles explains our use of the word "political" for them. The activist seeks to change hearts and minds and to fight (ideally in a fair way) for particular outcomes, often making considerable sacrifices to do so. Finally, the professional politician, as currently conceived, focuses mainly on "fighting" and not necessarily on "fighting fair." This role, in contrast to the other two, currently represents a degraded form of civic agency in contemporary discourse; one has to only glance at Congress's all-time-low approval ratings to recognize this.[28]

Each of these citizenly personae has some affinity with one of the models that Schudson analyzes as grounded in a particular historical era. The "civically engaged individual" has a close similarity to the Progressive Era's idealization of the "informed voter," the activist or political-entrepreneur with the civil rights era's rights-conscious citizen, and the "politician" with the late nineteenth-century model of the party loyalist. Yet, in our moment, all three of these models of civic agency—or updated versions of them—are elbowing and shoving one another in our public spheres. Given this fact, how do we educate for "participatory readiness"? Do we choose one of these models to emphasize? Or is there a way to integrate our understanding?

All three of these citizenly roles include "voting" in their responsibilities. But beyond that institutional responsibility, these roles develop very different conceptions of how to interact with both formal political institutions and the other levers that can be pulled to effect change.[29] They also develop very different conceptions of the types of speech and ethical orientations that should govern civic and political participation.[30] Each of these citizenly roles also presupposes a different approach to the development of intellectual and psychological capacities.

The civically engaged citizen who embraces the ideal of disinterested deliberation and pursues projects of "universal" value must, in some fashion, be clear about and counteract self-interest; must develop ways of testing whether things count as universal; and must absorb high-quality information on a wide array of issues.[31] The activist must be clear about interest and goals, must be good at strategic and tactical thinking, must understand "the levers of change," must be good at the techniques of storytelling that facilitate "frame shifting," and must have ethical parameters for thinking about the relationship between ends and means.[32] The professional politician, in the ideal, as opposed to in contemporary reality, would have both sets of the above competencies, as well as having expertise in how political institutions themselves function.

Notably, we have lost sight of the "ideal citizen" who combines success at all three citizenly tasks. That is, we have lost sight of the "statesman," who *is* a professional politician but who nonetheless has developed all the capacities described above as belonging to the other two roles and so is capable of disinterested deliberation, just "frame shifting," and fighting fair, as opposed to being capable merely of fighting.[33] But even more important, we have also lost sight of the "ordinary citizen," who is not a professional politician but who has nonetheless developed all the competencies described above and who is proud to be involved in "politics."

If we are to embrace an education for "participatory readiness," we need to aim our pedagogic and curricular work not at any single one of these three models, but at what lies behind all of them: a more fundamental understanding of what politics is. I embrace an Arendtian account of political life as something positive that consists of the activity of cocreating a way of life.[34] Ultimately, I think that this view of politics generates an account of "participatory readiness" that supports all three models of citizenship: the civically engaged individual, the activist, and the politician. It supports all three roles because each carries out only a subset of the work that constitutes public action. An education that prepares a student for Arendtian action should nourish future civic leaders, activists, *and* politicians. But such an education ought to also permit a reintegration of these role types. As we consider what sorts of pedagogies and curricula can achieve participatory readiness, then we have available two possible courses of action. We might direct an education for "participatory readiness" toward the three citizenly personae simultaneously, albeit as distinct and separable, or we might direct that education toward a reintegrated concept of civic agency. Either way, pursuing "participatory readiness" is an ambitious project and requires a much more expansive approach to "civic education" than I have yet to see exemplified.

THE CONTENT OF PARTICIPATORY READINESS

What should be the content of an education for "participatory readiness"? An aspiration to answer this question is visible in the June 2013 report called

"The Heart of the Matter," released by the Commission on the Humanities and Social Sciences established by Congress and organized by the American Academy of Arts and Sciences.[35] This report declared its first goal to be to "educate Americans in the knowledge, skills, and understanding they will need to thrive in a twenty-first-century democracy."[36] With this formulation, the "Heart of the Matter" report sought to rectify the gap in our public justification for the system of education by restoring a civic component. What is education for? It is for thriving in "democracy," not merely a global economy. So the report argues.

In the subsequent sections of the report, the commission detailed the activities for which it thought students should ready themselves. Drawing, among other sources, on the good work of litigator Michael Rebell and the Campaign for Fiscal Equity, the commission followed its goal statement with a recommendation: "The Commission therefore recommends a new dedication to 'participatory readiness' as an educational goal. We urge a nationwide commitment to preparing K–12 students for full participation in a democratic society. The Commission commends the Common Core State Standards Initiative for its inclusion of history and civics in the basic literacy curriculum. It promotes the competencies necessary for full civic participation in American society: voting, serving on juries, interpreting current events, developing respect for and understanding of differences, along with an ability to articulate one's sense of the common good."[37]

The commission adopted the language of "participatory readiness," but in its account of the education that achieves this, sketched the contours of civic education largely as we have traditionally known it. This traditional conception focuses on instruction in history and civics, primarily understood as classroom learning about the mechanics of government. Conventionally described as the "how a bill becomes a law" version of civic education, this approach prepares students for "informed" or "dutiful" citizenship as the media scholar Lance Bennett calls it.[38] This "informed citizen" model is what comes through most strongly in the Commission's report.

Yet in the passage quoted above, the commission—on which I need to confess that I served—did extend the basic civic education framework modestly and in two directions in particular. The report drew attention to the pressing need to prepare students to interact in conditions of diversity and also to the importance of developing in them linguistic competence adequate to offering up compelling visions of the public good. These are extensions on which I believe we can and should build.

There are two problems with the traditional "how a bill becomes a law" approach to civic education, at which the commission's report only hints.

First, to focus on the mechanics of government as the heart of civic education is to focus on only on a part of what is needed for the development of participatory readiness. Civic agents do need to understand the strategies and tactics available for bringing about political change, and the structure of political institutions is a part of this. But tactical knowledge is only one of the developmental pillars necessary for civic agency. In addition to tactical and strategic understanding, just as the commission suggests, students also need *verbal empowerment* and *democratic knowledge.* These are the two other developmental pillars supporting civic agency. I'll return to both of those concepts in a moment. The second problem with a focus on the institutional mechanics of government as the heart of civic education is that, even as an account of the tactics and strategies of civic agency, it is a limited picture, particularly in this era of new media and a transformed communications landscape. In sum, "participatory readiness" rests on three developmental pillars: verbal empowerment, democratic knowledge, and a rich understanding of the strategies and tactics that undergird efficacy. I'll turn to each of these pillars of "participatory readiness" in turn.

First, we turn to verbal empowerment. Verbal empowerment consists of interpretive (or exegetical) and expressive skills. Civic and political action must begin from a diagnosis of our current situation and move from that diagnosis to a prescription for a response. Such interpretive work, or in the language of the Declaration of Independence, the work of reading "the course of human events," can be done only in and through language. Data are only one subset of the linguistic resources available to this work of diagnosis and prescription. Conversational work is necessary to clarify the meaning of data—regardless of how big those data are. The analytical skills that constitute acts of interpretation only ever manifest themselves in language: diagnoses of particular circumstances and prescriptions of what is to be done.

Moreover, success at the movement from diagnosis to prescription requires not merely the verbal skills embodied in acts of interpretation but also expressive skills. For these social diagnoses to become effective, one must convince others of them. The verbal work involved in civic agency extends well beyond our usual focus on deliberation to include adversarial and pro-phetic speech also. This component of "participatory readiness" used to be taught, from antiquity through the nineteenth century, under the heading of rhetoric.[39]

Second, "participatory readiness" requires what I, building on the work of classicist and political scientist, Josiah Ober, call "democratic knowledge." Democracy is an egalitarian political form, and one of the great paradoxes of egalitarianism is that it functions not through a reduction or diminishment of the need for leadership but through its increase. Democracies spawn vast numbers of collective decision-making bodies. The Athenians famously had a long list of boards of administrators and civic officers, many populated by lottery. In the case of the United States, during the period of the Revolution-ary War, the Continental Congress scarcely went a day without setting up committees to carry out congressional business.[40] The French aristocrat and intellectual Alexis de Tocqueville, who traveled in the United States in the 1830s, noticed how prolific nineteenth-century Americans were at forming associations, and despite political scientist Robert Putnam's tales in *Bowling Alone* of decline in the twentieth century, we in fact continue to be very busy in this regard.[41] Our forms of association have certainly changed, and for very good reasons, among them that the law of association was fundamentally re-structured between 1970 and 1990, but it is by no means clear that associa-tions are any less common now than at earlier points. (In other words, I think Putnam's story is fundamentally wrong, an issue I address elsewhere.[42])

All this associating generates its own science and demands its own art form.[43] Call these simply the science and art of association. I call this sci-ence and art—taken together, "democratic knowledge"—because they pin-point bodies of knowledge that grow up in democratic contexts, specifically. While there are many components to this science and art of association, I consider among the most important to be its relational elements. On this front, democratic knowledge consists of what I call cosmopolitan bonding skills, on the one hand, and bridging skills on the other. The latter is easier to understand. These bridging skills consist of the capacities by which a trans-lator, a mediator, and an individual who can surmount social difference can convert a costly social relationship into one that is mutually beneficial to both parties. Cosmopolitan bonding skills, in contrast, relate to the precise nature of the bonds that we form with the people to whom we feel the most affinity, whether that is because of shared kinship, geographical collocation, ethnicity, religion, or similarity of preferences. For the sake of healthy psychological development, all people need bonding relationships.[44] But not all bonding relationships are the same. We need to bond in ways that help preserve the democracy of which we are a part.[45] Indeed, the question of how we bond is deeply entangled with the question of whether we are able to bridge.[46] Thus the critical question for a democratic society is how we can bond with those who are like us so as to help us bridge even with those who differ from us. In order for any method of bonding—for instance, that which begins from social homogeneity or that which begins from interest affinity—to support our capacity to bridge, the very experience of bonding must cultivate receptivity toward the potential of participation in our bonding group by social dissimilars. The question of just what sorts of styles and methods of social bonding can be cosmopolitan in this way is a difficult one, which I will not address in this book.[47] It is sufficient for our purposes simply to mark out the terrain by identifying this, too, as a core component of "participatory readiness." Cosmopolitan bonding skills and bridging skills are both necessary for civic actors to function effectively across political institutions and other spaces for political action. They are also necessary for the formation of solidarity that supports civic and political action outside of institutions.

Finally, verbal empowerment and the acquisition of democratic knowledge require supplementation by tactical and strategic understanding or knowledge of the mechanics of political action. As I have mentioned, this last area is where civic and political education has traditionally focused. The error in focusing here is, of course, the failure to take the domains of verbal empowerment and democratic knowledge fully into account. But there is also another problem with the traditional focus on the mechanics of government—this one stemming from the transformation of public spheres in our new media age. Traditionally, we have thought about this "tactical" part of civic education as requiring lessons in how a bill becomes a law, but a feature of our new media age is that levers of change outside of political institutions are now easier to pull.[48] Consequently, tactical and strategic understanding now also requires learning about how civic agents can interact with corporations and nongovernmental organizations or as part of social movements. It requires understanding how cultural norms can be changed and how changes in cultural norms bring about broader political changes.[49] It also requires understanding a new architecture of communication. Where once we needed to know how to write letters to the editor and to Congress, now we need to master the architecture and rhetorics of the Internet and social media.[50] We still have a curricular and pedagogic need for the traditional focus of civic education on the Constitution and structure of government, but this domain of strategies and tactics now requires expansion. And of course there is also the question of the ethical norms that should guide our deployment of these strategies and tactics.

The core elements of "participatory readiness," then, are as follows: verbal empowerment; strategic and tactical understanding of the levers of political change, broadly conceived, and the ethics of their use; and democratic, associational know-how. This is a nonexhaustive account of the elements of "participatory readiness," but these are, I think, the most significant human capacities that require cultivation if each of us is to be well prepared to function as a civic and political actor. Admittedly, these goals convey a lofty— even utopian—aspiration, but it's good to aim high, and well-crafted ideals should help us make choices even about small steps that we take.

CULTIVATING PARTICIPATORY READINESS

How can we cultivate capacities of these kinds? What small steps might we take? For the rest of this chapter, I will limit my focus to the relationship between "participatory readiness" and verbal empowerment. As mentioned previously, this is not the only component of participatory readiness or civic agency. There is also room for action, performance, and even joyful play. But I think we have in recent years paid too little attention to the importance of verbal empowerment, and I hope to redress that. As I focus on verbal empowerment and its contributions to participatory readiness, we will soon find that the unlikely hero of my story is the humanities, or a liberal arts education. We will also finally see the significance of using the humanistic baseline to define education as it pertains to the actual teaching of actual students.

In the vast universe of educational data, one can catch fleeting glimpses here and there of an answer to the question of how teachers can cultivate "participatory readiness." For instance, it's clear that college provides something useful there that our K–12 system generally does not.

As the philosopher of education Meira Levinson and others have pointed out, educational attainment is a better predictor of the likelihood of voting

TABLE 1. *Percentage of US citizens over eighteen who voted in*
2004 and 2008 presidential elections by educational attainment

Educational attainment	2004 election	2008 election
Less than high school diploma	40 percent	39 percent
High school graduate	56 percent	55 percent
Some college or associate's degree	69 percent	68 percent
Bachelor's degree	78 percent	77 percent
Advanced degree	84 percent	83 percent

Data from Levinson 2012, p. 35, calculated from US Census Bureau, "Voting and Registration in the Election of November 2004—Detailed Tables" and "Voting and Registration in the Election of November 2008—Detailed Tables."

than even income (table 1).[51] In other words, although we don't talk terribly often or in very consistent ways about how college provides a civic and political education, something is happening on our campuses that engenders "participatory readiness." What colleges achieve is not even close to the whole package that I've laid out above, and colleges generally serve young men better than young women when it comes to the development of leadership skills.[52] Moreover, insofar as colleges succeed in generating participatory readiness, a significant part of that success surely derives from the preparation of students for economic success.[53] After all, those with property have a great deal at stake in the decisions of political institutions and are therefore quite likely to be engaged. Yet this is not the whole of the story. There is a closer correlation between level of educational attainment and likelihood of voting than even between socioeconomic status and likelihood of voting, so something is at work here *other* than socioeconomic status. But what is it? And can we build on it? Socioeconomic status is so powerful in its impact on educational outcomes for specific individuals and on political participation that we ought to work hard, I think, to build on any faint glimmer of possibility where one can see positive educational developments, positive developments toward civic empowerment, that have actually broken the connection to socioeconomic status. This is what I will seek to do in what follows.

There is also an important corollary to the observation that college makes a meaningful difference for "participatory readiness." If those who have advanced degrees vote more than those with college degrees, and those with college degrees more than those with high school degrees, we have what Levinson has called a civic achievement gap. If the goal of an educational system is to achieve participatory readiness for all students, this is an element of our education that we should hope to bring to satisfactory level by age eighteen, the age of political majority. The civic achievement gap means we're not doing well enough in the K–12 system in cultivating "participatory readiness."

Beyond socioeconomic effects, then, what exactly is happening on college campuses and not in the K–12 system that might be contributing to the difference here? Not all college is the same, of course, and this fact holds an important key (table 2). Students have varying experiences depending, among other things, on their choice of major. Interestingly, there is a statistically significant difference between the rates of political participation that we see from those who have graduated with humanities majors and those who graduate with STEM (science, technology, engineering, and mathematics) majors.

Similarly, participation in social science college curricula is a strong predictor of later political participation, according to Duke University political scientist Sunshine Hillygus.[54] Hillygus conducted the study to control for the possibility of self-selection of those with civic and political interests into social sciences courses, and even with this control in place, she found an effect on later political participation from enrollment in social science courses. Her paper provides strong evidence for a correlation between work in the humanities and social sciences and participatory readiness.

TABLE 2. *Not all college is the same*

	Humanities	STEM
Ever voted as of one year out (class of 2008)	92.8 percent	83.5 percent
Wrote to public officials by ten years out (class of 1993)	44.1 percent	30.1 percent

College graduates' civic engagement. Data from the American Academy of Arts and Sciences. Figures calculated using US Department of Education, National Center for Education Statistics, B&B: 08/09 Baccalaureate and Beyond Longitudinal Study; B&B: 93/03 Baccalaureate and Beyond Longitudinal Study.

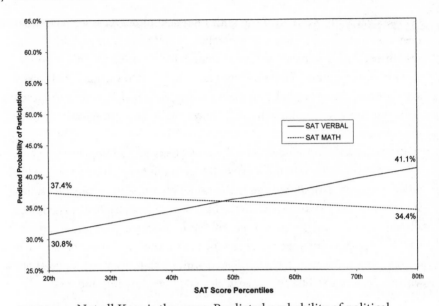

FIGURE 1. Not all K–12 is the same: Predicted probability of political participation by SAT percentiles
From Hillygus 2005, p. 39. Reprinted with permission from Springer Science+ Business Media Inc.

The difference between different educational strands in higher education is mirrored in K–12 education. Just as those who major in the humanities or take social science courses in college are more likely to participate politically after graduation, so too those whose verbal skills are higher by the end of high school, as measured by SATs, are more likely to become active political participants than those with high math scores. Moreover, the SAT effect endures even when college-level curricular choices are controlled for (figure 1).

To identify a correlation is not, of course, to identify causation, but those with more sophisticated verbal skills are clearly more ready to be civic and political participators. This may be because another source of motivation engaged them in politics, and then, once they were engaged, these students sought the verbal skills that they needed to thrive in the domain of political participation. Or the verbal ability may make it easier to engage. We don't have a study that considers levels of engagement before and after significant increases in verbal ability. Nonetheless, what we do have in data such as these is a tantalizing suggestion that the work of the humanities on verbal empowerment is intrinsically related to the development of "participatory readiness." Explaining just how is an important and largely unaddressed research question.[55]

In addition to the data points that one can find scattered here and there as provocative clues to a profound story about the humanities, language, and participatory readiness, one also finds occasional anecdotes that help elucidate the connection between language and civic agency. In a volume called *Citizenship across the Curriculum*, Rebecca Nowacek, an English professor, relates the following story about the discovery by one humanities student of how her major had distinctively prepared her to participate in public life:

> Early in the collaborative process [of working with two classmates on the knotty local problem of school choice within Milwaukee public schools], an English major told me she felt that the value of her disciplinary knowledge was questioned, even slighted. One of her groupmates was a political science major, well versed in questions of public policy. The other was a speech pathologist, with experience working in the local schools. What could someone who sits reading novels bring to their collaborative inquiry? Whether their skepticism was real or only imagined, the English major felt the need to articulate for her groupmates—and for herself—what her studies of literature had prepared her to contribute to the understanding of this knotty local problem. . . .
>
> Ultimately she determined that what she could contribute to her group was her capacity to identify and tease out the significance of patterns in discourse. She conducted a careful reading of local newspaper coverage of school choice, identifying a number of disturbing trends.[56]

This English major's heightened linguistic sensitivity was her special skill. My contention here is that it is also the foundational civic competency. It's the English major who was in a position to diagnose what was actually happening in the community and the meanings of how particular choices were being framed. We see her interpretive skills at work. We also see her expressive skills. She "felt the need to articulate . . . what her studies of literature had prepared her to contribute," and in response to this need, she was able to develop and express a memorable answer. The anecdote is too partial for us to know just what political meaning the English major found in the newspaper or to know precisely how she contributed to the world making in which she was engaged alongside the political science and speech pathology majors. Yet we do see in this anecdote a deployment of the first political skill: diagnosis. Notably, reading novels—interpreting them—was what had prepared this student for her own life of action in the Arendtian sense.

This investigation of the relationship between the humanities, verbal empowerment, and participatory readiness is nothing more than a suggestive gesture toward precisely how we might cultivate participatory readiness. If verbal empowerment is at the base of political empowerment, and if the humanities have a special impact there, then we have a case for the humanities in their potential to contribute to "participatory readiness." I have, in other words, in my pursuit of the links between education and equality, wandered into a defense of the humanities. This is because of the potential of education to advance political equality, a potentiality that is closely connected, I suggest, to humanistic components of the curriculum.

My suggestion is that the humanistic components of the curriculum do a distinctive kind of work in support of participatory readiness and that this work does not directly correlate with the socioeconomic status effects of education on participation. Why is it important to emphasize how the humanities help cultivate participatory readiness when the effects may seem quite small in comparison to the impacts of socioeconomic status on life course? As I mentioned above, socioeconomic status is so powerful that one needs to tap into every available resource for counteracting its effects. The role of the humanities and verbal empowerment is not a complete solution, but it would be foolish to leave aside a genuine resource that is evidently available. Moreover, what are small effects now could be larger effects down the road if we seriously consider the connection that Hillygus, for instance, has identified and refocus pedagogy around the insights about verbal empowerment that I have tried to develop.

To conclude my argument, though, I'd like to complete these thoughts about the relationship between education and equality. The link that I have suggested among the humanities, language, and participatory readiness brings us to what I think is at the heart of education's egalitarian force. Education's most fundamental egalitarian value is in its development of us as language-using creatures. Our linguistic capacities are what education fundamentally taps, and it is their great unfolding that empowers students. This verbal empowerment prepares us for participation in civic and political life. As we cultivate verbal empowerment in our students, we build the foundation for a politically competitive social and political system. We have good reason to expect that a genuinely competitive political system would put matters of economic fairness into play for contestation. This returns us to the idea that by supporting political equality, educational institutions themselves can affect "how technology evolves, how markets function, and how the gains from various different economic arrangements are distributed."[57] The idea is that there ought to be a developmental "threshold"—identified here as the cultivation of participatory readiness—that enables human beings to compete politically even with others who have achieved a higher level of educational attainment. The fundamental relationship between education and equality, then, is that the very definition of education rests on a conception of shared human capacities, which, when fully activated, have the potential (by supporting political equality) to move us toward a world that reduces or eliminates the positional aspect of the good of education itself. Consequently, the most valuable way for us to direct our educational system toward egalitarian ends may be by focusing on participatory readiness. Finally, I would suggest that it is perhaps because we have lost sight of the contributions made by the humanities to our educational system that we have also lost sight of the fundamental link between education and equality that I have tried to clarify.

CONCLUSION

Let me, then, offer a brief conclusion. The great beauty of language's power as a catalyst of human capacity is that we all have access to it, so any of us can choose anywhere, anytime to plumb its depths and climb with it to the heights of human achievement. An adequately egalitarian educational system would maximally activate the latent capacities in the powerful, invisible body of language, which dwells inside each of us. Even when an educational system fails us, we still have access to self-development. We can educate ourselves, and many have. Before the arrival of compulsory education, there were Benjamin Franklin, Abraham Lincoln, Frederick Douglass, and Susan B. Anthony. After its arrival, there were the participants in the Freedom Schools in the South in the summer of 1964. There are also the

Clemente Courses, inspired by Earl Shorris and Sarah Hirschman's work on People and Stories, in which low-income adults achieve personal empowerment by improving their capacity to diagnose their circumstances and present convincing arguments to others about new directions to pursue.[58] When we strip our idea of education of the state apparatus—that is, of the system-level concept—we see again that what remains is what I have been calling the humanistic baseline, the idea that education begins as an effort to unfold or awaken the powers that mark us as human, the first of which is language. Any of us in any social circumstance can undertake this awakening. In this fact, we come back to a fundamental human equality and also to the political equality that language opens up as a possibility for us. We come back to the human capacity, latent in our linguistic power, for world making—through work and play, political contestation and prophesy, art and deliberation. And we come back to the possibility that the cultivation of participatory readiness leads to political institutions that will themselves pull toward social equality and economic fairness.

] Justification, Learning,
and Human Flourishing
Tommie Shelby

INTRODUCTION

The explicit primary concern of Danielle Allen's argument is the relationship between education as an institution and equality as an ideal (or, better, a set of related ideals). But there is a lot more of interest in these rich and provocative essays. I find much in Allen's vision of education to be compelling, and I agree with many of her conclusions about the relationship between education and equality. I am particularly drawn to her important contention that education has a role to play in preparing individuals for civic engagement and political participation (and not just to facilitate public deliberation) and that this can, at least indirectly, address problems of inequality.

I do, however, have reservations about some dimensions of the outlook as presented. I take up three related issues. First, I will critically reflect on the general framework of justification that Allen relies on. Next, I will raise some questions about her approach to resolving the debate over the place of the liberal arts or humanities in education. Finally, I will draw attention to the notes of political perfectionism in her account with a view to highlighting the advantages of an alternative liberal egalitarian framework.

JUSTIFICATION

Allen believes that we cannot fully grasp the relation between education and equality without a clear grasp of *what education fundamentally is*. With this understanding firmly established, we will then be able to see the *intrinsic* relation between education and equality—the way in which the two are inextricably linked conceptually (if not in practice). She highlights the tendency in public discourse to treat education as a remedy for poverty or economic inequality. But she insists that this merely contingent connection between education and equality can't reveal to us why education *itself* is valuable. This way of framing the issue suggests that education has a discoverable *essence*, a feature that makes it what it is and that is present wherever education (properly understood) is occurring. As she argues, education is, essentially, the *social practice of human development.*

Allen might be right about what education essentially involves. What I want to focus on, though, is how she arrives at this conclusion—the justificatory scheme she employs to establish it. She moves from *conceptual truths* (maybe even *metaphysical truths*) about education as a social practice to fixing the fundamental *practical goals* of education. Notice the approach to normative inquiry: Start with the question "What is X?" (or "What is the nature of X?"). Then proceed from an answer to that question to explaining the *value* of X (to explain why X is worthwhile).

Drawing our attention to processes of institutional development, Allen argues that once a social practice has differentiated itself from all others, its internal logic emerges or becomes manifest, and from this logic, we derive its normative principles. Sometimes these autonomous social practices are transformed into sociopolitical practices—that is, public officials take control of the practice and maintain authority over it. Allen claims that when this happens, state officials should regulate the practice in accordance with the practice's internal logic and its corresponding practical principles. The essence of the practice is thus, at least partly, *prescriptive.* Knowing what education is constrains how its institutionalization is to be structured.

Relying on Rawls, Allen distinguishes two types of justification for education. At the *macro*level, there is an end that justifies the state's maintenance of a system of education (system-level justification). At the *micro*level, there is a justification for particular acts of educating within the system (action-specific justification). It is only at the microlevel, action-specific justification that we discover the essence of education. It is also at this level that concrete needs of *individuals* (as opposed to the general welfare of society) are addressed.

Allen acknowledges that at the level of system justification, education can have different, historically contingent purposes—aims that can be utilitarian (e.g., promoting economic competitiveness). But the common activity within all these practices, whatever their system-level justification, is *cultivating human capacities.* This activity, the very substance of teaching, cannot have a utilitarian justification, she insists. What all the different educational institutions have in common, despite their different purposes, is the "aspiration to direct the development of human capacities."

How does Allen know that the microlevel justification for education is human development for its own sake? She identifies the essence of education, its fundamental purpose, by isolating that end that all forms of education have in common and that education alone can secure. And this leads her to endorse what she calls the humanistic baseline: the principle that education essentially involves developing human capacities as valuable in itself.

My first question about this framework of justification is why we should think that social practices, even those institutionalized by the state, have "logics" that can be discovered by tracing their history or by discerning their essence. I am not just being a nit-picking philosopher who thinks that talk of "logic" should be reserved for inferential relations between propositions or the study of valid reasoning. Rather, I do not think I fully understand the social theory operating in the background, especially since I am doubtful that Allen is presupposing a structuralist understanding of practices. So one way of presenting the first part of my concern is with this question: Are we to think that each autonomous social practice has a function and a set of organizing principles that exist apart from the purposes of and the rules laid down by those who establish, participate in, and rely on these practices, and if so, why? This is largely a request to have the social-theoretic assumptions behind the vision made explicit.

But let's suppose we have that theory in hand. What would be the normative import of such a theory? How are we to understand its prescriptive force? Suppose I am someone who thinks that the day-to-day activity of teaching should always be aimed at worker readiness. Why should I change my mind if I discover that human development for its own sake is the end that only education can serve? After all, some practices serve ends that are not worthwhile—or at least not worth the public funds spent on them. If I am told that all educational institutions (which are properly called this) develop human capacities, why should I conclude from this fact (if it is a fact) that teachers must value cultivating such capacities for its own sake?

Let me add a few other comments and questions on this theme. First, I must confess that I am not entirely sure why Allen thinks the common activity within educational institutions could not have a utilitarian justification—why, that is, the rules that govern pedagogy and curriculum could not derive their normative force from the system-level aim. It might be, as a practical matter, that teachers could not do a good job cultivating marketable talents if their day-to-day instruction was always geared toward producing this result. The kids might not respond well to instruction if their teachers treat them like raw materials in a manufacturing process. But I suspect that this is a different issue from the one animating Allen.

Nor do I see why the specific activities that occur within the educational system could not also have diverse purposes. Why must there be some common end that they all serve? And even if they do all have (at some abstract level) the same end, I am not convinced that this end has to be the development of human capacities. Another aim that all education seems to have in common is *learning through formal instruction*. I will return to this point about learning in a moment.

So it is fair to ask, what is an alternative model of justification? How else might we justify education without reducing it to its instrumental value for social welfare or employment? I think of the justification of social practices as something we offer to others (and sometimes that we owe to others) when we stand (or could stand) in certain relations to them, particularly when a practice we support deeply affects their basic interests. So we justify punishment to those we punish or to those vulnerable to punishment, as well as to those we require to pay for the practice or to participate in it.

To fill in this conception a bit, it might make sense to unpack Rawls's notion of an institution as a system of rules.[1] (Allen suggests that she is "riffing" on Rawls's famous distinction, so perhaps she doesn't accept the details of his account of how to justify an institution or social practice. Still, making some of the details of Rawls's framework explicit could be helpful here.) According to Rawls, an institution's structure is defined by a *system of rules* that define offices, roles, permissions, duties, procedures, penalties, exemptions, and so on within a social practice. The system as a whole can be justified by how these public rules, taken together, promote some worthy end (e.g., democratic accountability, public health, social order, lasting peace). The particular rules within a practice, taken individually, need not all be justified in terms of how they are directly instrumental to the practice-justifying end. Nor must these internal rules all have the same justification. Some rules are there, for example, to ensure fairness to participants and to those excluded from participating. Some rules are there to ensure that power is exercised wisely and not abused. Some rules might exist simply to incentivize participation and good conduct. Some might serve mainly to enhance efficiency.

So when we ask what justifies a role-defining rule, procedure, or permission within a school, the answer we give might differ depending on the type of rule in question. And because there are various roles within a school (administrator, teacher, coach, tutor, bus driver, janitor, crossing guard, etc.), the roles themselves might have different justifications. Even within a given role, say that of teacher, just what properly defines the role (its duties and permissions) may depend on a host of considerations. In short, the micro-level justification of particular actions within an institution can be complex.

Now, Allen might ask, given how different any two institutions can be in terms of their system-level aims and constitutive rules, how are we to know when an institution is properly regarded as an *educational* institution and not something else (say, a mere vocational program or recreational center)? Honestly, I would not know how to answer that question. But if our primary concern is with *justification* rather than metaphysics, we might say something along the following lines.

We could start by noting that learning through instruction can be valuable (both to students and to society) and that, given its value, we should sometimes create or sustain public institutions that specialize in it. Allen starts with education as a formal social practice, a state-controlled institution that mediates relations between students and teachers. She tries to discern the internal logic and organizing principle of this institution to figure out what it's good for. But we might instead focus on human beings as *learners*. We can then ask what is important to learn and why. (There probably won't be a single answer to the why question.) Among the many things worth learning, we can select those things that are reasonable for the state to ensure (through regulation and public funding) that everyone (or some people) learn. Against this background, we could ask what institutional structures would, in a cost-effective way, best ensure that this learning takes place. And if we were taking up questions of educational reform, our question would be how these institutions (or alternative ones) could do this job better.

This way of framing the issue of justification does not, in itself, deliver a rebuttal to the argument that however valuable learning for its own sake is, the public should not be burdened with paying for it, given how expensive and time-consuming such learning can be and how (much more) important it is that individuals learn things that are socially useful and will earn them income. But, as I have indicated, I am not sure that Allen's approach provides the necessary traction either.

HUMANISTIC KNOWLEDGE

This leads me to a comment on the debate over the humanities. As Allen rightly notes, so much of the current discourse focuses on the development of socially useful talents (or on talents that, when developed, are marketable) and on the acquisition of knowledge that might make the knower valuable to others. Allen's approach to resolving the debate between the neoliberals and the champions of the liberal arts is to invoke two concepts of education (the two-level justificatory framework), charging these two would-be adversaries with confusing these two concepts.

I agree entirely that the public debate over education is not best framed in terms of vocational training versus liberal arts, as if these were diametrically opposed alternatives in a fight where we must all choose sides. But those, like me, who are concerned about the fate of liberal arts education are worried about at least two issues. First, we fear that vocational training is effectively crowding out the liberal arts in terms of the time and resources devoted to each, and second, we are concerned that the liberal arts will be widely seen to have value only insofar as they increase students' job-related skills (e.g., enhancing critical, analytical, problem-solving, interpretive, public-speaking, and writing skills).

In light of this substantive disagreement, I am inclined to think that the proper terrain for public debate is not over what education fundamentally is. Rather, the debate should focus on the relative importance of learning job-related skills versus learning other things and on the extent to which public (and private) money and instruction time should be devoted to these various forms of learning. I do not see how the two-concepts framework helps resolve this debate in a way that gives proper weight to the concerns of those who value the liberal arts. Indeed, the focus on *human development* might actually exacerbate the problem.

The reason is that this focus on developing human capacities sets up a different conflict, one between the cultivation of *skills* and the acquisition of *knowledge*. Not all knowledge is practical know-how. And even when knowledge does enable the knower to do things she could not do before, this increase in skill is often a by-product, not an aim, of the instruction. Instruction, if done well, will effect a change in the pupil—the student will learn something worth knowing. However, the knowledge gained, to be worthwhile, need not increase the pupil's abilities. Must there be some not fully realized capacity that gets further developed in the process of learning? I do not see why. The pupil may not be able to *do* anything with the knowledge, and the knowledge acquired is not degraded by its lack of practical usefulness.

Of course, Allen has an expansive conception of the skills that education (properly understood) must cultivate. Her vision of education is not limited to developing our capacities for making things or providing services that others find useful. She is equally and rightly concerned that students acquire the skills necessary for productive civic engagement and political participation. And certainly one of the things that, say, studying Plato's dialogues or Toni Morrison's novels can do for a student is enable her to be a more fully realized political agent through the enhancement of her verbal skills.

However, part of what the embattled champion of the liberal arts is after, I take it, is an educational system that does not reduce all instruction to *training*—the cultivation of useful skills. I do not just mean skills that are useful to others or that the market will remunerate; I also mean to include skills that are practically useful only to the one who possesses them.

Allen views education as fundamentally *preparation for a flourishing life*. But talk of "preparation" or "readiness" makes education sound mostly like training for something the student might do in the future—whether earning a living, participating in politics, cultivating loving relationships, or creating things of value. They are being *equipped* to do something later in life.

The champion of the liberal arts could respond by insisting that education satisfies *current* needs of students—for example, the need for self-understanding, the need to satisfy one's curiosity about the world, the need to correct one's mistaken judgments about other people, the need to grasp the sublime. We are not just doers but *knowers*, and knowledge brings its own satisfaction—even if contemplation isn't the highest form of life or the most worthwhile activity. In short, I do not see how valuing knowledge for its own sake fits into a conception of human flourishing as the development of our distinctive capacities.

As a highly knowledgeable lover of poetry and theatre, Allen surely understands (much better than I, in fact) that the value of the humanities goes well beyond how it enhances students' skill set (however broadly "skill" is understood). Perhaps what she is after is a rapprochement between neo-liberal pragmatists and idealistic advocates for the humanities, a resolution that both sides can live with and that is compatible with democratic ideals. If so, I welcome and am grateful for her intervention. But I also hold out the hope that a more full-throated defense of the liberal arts is available, a defense that both highlights the distinctive value of humanistic knowledge and can garner broad public support.

DEMOCRACY AND THE HUMAN GOOD

Allen could argue that, despite her focus on "readiness," the kind of preparation she has in mind cannot be reduced to training, because the skills enhancement is done for its own sake, not to shape students to play any particular social role. Teaching, in her view, *empowers* students to play a wide range of roles in social life. I find this aspect of her account compelling. Yet there are perfectionist elements in her vision that prevent me from fully endorsing it. Specifically, her framework raises issues about the role of state power when dealing with citizens who have conflicting conceptions of the good.

Recall that Allen integrates the system-level justification of education with the action-specific justification by relying on Arendt's account of human flourishing. Given the Arendtian account of the human good, education should cultivate four capacities: our capacities for work, for political participation, for creativity, and for forming and sustaining fulfilling social relationships. This democratic-eudaemonistic interpretation of the humanistic baseline is intrinsically connected to *equality*, Allen argues, because it requires that all education meet the same set of human needs for all students. It turns out that when the state uses the educational system to promote economic growth and a healthy democracy (system-level justification), it thereby promotes human flourishing in all individual students (action-specific justification).

However, when we talk of *human needs*, it can be difficult to give a convincing account of what these are beyond the requirements for survival and full health. Given what we know about Homo sapiens, we might extend this to a conception of basic human well-being, both physical and psychological. Beyond this, we get into highly contested terrain, all the more so when the "needs" in question are regarded as requirements for human happiness. Again, I am doubtful that what it means to flourish comes down to a conceptual truth or empirical fact. It is, I believe, an irreducible normative question, and so only normative considerations can settle it (if anything can).

For instance, contrary to what Arendt suggests, working to earn a living is not a basic human need. Individuals, as a biological matter, do not need to be economically self-sufficient. They of course need food, clothing, shelter, and so on. But how they gain access to these material goods will depend on how the society in question is structured. In a just, wealthy society, some might get these things without laboring so as to "earn" them. (There is also a concern here about implicitly devaluing socially valuable work that the market will not compensate—for example, a lot of dependency work, including child-rearing.) Moreover, I would not myself endorse economic self-sufficiency as an ideal of the good. Preparation to contribute one's share to the material reproduction of society seems far better. This, however, would be a matter of economic fairness and civic reciprocity, not of individual flourishing.

Relatedly, Allen thinks that *teachers* must regard the cultivation of their students' abilities as valuable in itself. But what about the students? What do we say to the students (or to their parents) who instrumentalize their own capacities regarding their development as valuable only insofar as it makes them competitive in the labor market or returns high income? Does democratic eudaemonism imply that they do not understand what it means to truly flourish? And what would be the practical implications of this lack of understanding? Should teachers try to get their students to appreciate the intrinsic value of human development? Should public funds be expended and compulsory education used to get students to come around to this appreciation? What I am attempting to highlight with these questions is the role of *ideals of the human good* in public deliberation about the structure and aims of education.

In addition to earning a living through work, Allen regards participation in politics as a component of human flourishing (our need to cocreate our shared life), and so education should equip us to realize ourselves as political agents. I also think that preparation for participation in public life is important and that schools have a crucial role to play in this. However, I am reluctant to attempt to justify this role in terms of democratic eudaemonism or any conception of human flourishing. I would say instead that we each have a duty to help create and sustain just institutions and social relations. To fulfill this duty of justice, we need to prepare ourselves, as a matter of political ethics, to play this role effectively, which may include reforming educational institutions so that they contribute to (or at least do not thwart) the cultivation of the relevant political skills.

As an advocate of political liberalism, I am inclined to think that state power and public funds can permissibly be used to enable citizens to devise and revise their conceptions of human flourishing and to empower citizens to achieve their fundamental purposes in life.[2] I am skeptical of government attempts to determine for citizens what constitutes human flourishing and to direct citizens toward what state officials regard as good for them.

I think it is consistent with political liberalism to view education as an activity that broadens students' horizons so that they can discover which of their talents it makes sense to cultivate in light of both the satisfaction it brings them to exercise the talent and the social opportunities available to them for exercising it (and perhaps to be paid and recognized for doing so).

Education can also expose students to ideals of life that they might make their own. There are conceptions of the good life (conceptions of human flourishing) that students should be exposed to, not just to cultivate tolerance for difference (and thus good citizenship), but to help students determine if they might find satisfaction in adopting these conceptions for their own lives.

In contrast to political liberalism, democratic eudaemonism conceptualizes education in a way that implies a fixed path toward a predetermined end, an ideal of human self-realization. Democratic eudaemonism treats human capacities as potential that can be fulfilled, wasted, and maybe even perverted. It suggests that if our educational institutions are not cultivating all our distinctive human capacities for the sake of having them developed, then they are not really educating students. Maybe this is all correct. That is, maybe Allen, with the help of Aristotle and Arendt, has identified the truly human good. Nevertheless, I doubt that educational accountability is best cast in such terms within a pluralist democratic society.

CONCLUSION

As I mentioned at the start, I agree with many of the conclusions in Allen's terrifically interesting and challenging argument. My concerns are largely with how she arrives at them—the mode of justification that she employs. In some ways, the doubts I have expressed can be viewed as an invitation to Allen. They are an invitation to say more about her preference for a Platonist framework of normative justification over, say, a contractualist mode of justification and an invitation to make explicit the background social theory that animates her vision of education. They are an invitation to explain why those who champion the liberal arts should be satisfied with a conception of education as human development. And they are an invitation to make clear why she prefers neo-Aristotelian political perfectionism over political liberalism.

] A Reunion

Marcelo Suárez-Orozco

> We should think that we have more need of being nostalgic,
> not so much about the past but more nostalgic about the
> future. The children expect us in the future where our
> nostalgia now sees them and I wish we will all be there.
> —Loris Malaguzzi, "Speech in Acceptance of the Kohl
> Foundation International Teaching Award"

The 2014 Tanner Lectures, hosted by Stanford's McCoy Family Center for Ethics in Society and faithfully evoked in this volume, were a reunion of sorts. The reunion was literal: scholars and practitioners who over the years have collaborated with Danielle Allen came together again for a few memorable days at the Stanford campus.

But the reunion I have in mind is of a different sort.

Philosophers have left their place at education's table. The Tanner Lectures and this book, let us hope, begin to reclaim a place in education scholarship ceded by philosophers over the last six generations—first to psychologists and *pedagogistas* and then to economists, as the historian of education Ellen Lagemann and others have pointed out. Over 125 years ago, Émile Durkheim, then a studious disciple of the neo-Kantians Renouvier and Boutroux, and the historian Fustel de Coulanges began lecturing in Bourdeaux as would-be teachers about moral values and collective consciousness. By the time Durkheim was inducted into the Sorbonne's prestigious chair, he had found in education the articulation of what would become his enduring conceptual contribution to the social sciences: the nature of the relationships between the individual and society. "Very far from there being the antagonism between the individual and society which is often claimed, moral individualism, the cult of the individual, is in fact the product of society itself. It is society that instituted it and made of man the god whose servant it is."[1] Through education, society makes god of man.

In the Anglo-American tradition, the philosopher's place at education's table was equally weighty. In John Dewey's architecture, education mediates between the individual and the democratic ideal. In a passage echoing Durkheim's general sentiments, Dewey writes, "education is a regulation of the process of coming to share in the social consciousness; and that the adjustment of individual activity on the basis of this social consciousness is the only sure method of social reconstruction."[2] In the American tradition, Dewey set the tone during the critical formative years of education as a practice and field of inquiry. And, as Sussana Mantovani reminds us, there was a time when philosophy-savvy *pedagogistas* in the mold of Maria Montessori, Loris Malaguzzi, Paulo Freire, and others were powerful voices—if not always at the head of the table, certainly in a place of privilege.[3] So were psychologists like Lev Vygotsky, Jean Piaget, Jerome Bruner, and his students—Howard Gardner and others. Little by little, they also lost their place of privilege.

Today the privilege to set the tone of the table belongs to economists. It is the likes of James Heckman, Larry Katz and Claudia Goldin, Roland Fryer, and even Larry Summers—all at Harvard. MIT's David Autor and Stanford's Eric Hanushek command the most attention, if not at the barricades where education now more or less permanently lives,[4] then certainly in the circles closer to the *mana*—that indispensable Polynesian idea with no precise cognate in the Indo-European languages but vaguely related to power and authority.[5] Indisputably, with regard to education, philosophers have lost their place of privilege.[6] So the appearance of Allen's work is a significant new direction. That the publication of these Tanner Lectures will coincide with the hundredth anniversary of the publication of Dewey's *Democracy and Education* (and the 115th anniversary of Durkheim's Chair on Education Science at the Sorbonne) is yet another reunion of sorts. Let us hope it won't take another century for other philosophers to enter the conversation. Let us hope this is not a fleeting rendezvous. Let us hope philosophy is back for the long run.

The shift in who is at the table toasting which ideas is part and parcel of the changing zeitgeist. Our shared preoccupations, priorities, and ambitions for the purposes of education are decidedly fluid and not always harmonious—a process both Dewey and Durkheim well understood. The context in which free and compulsory public education came to be a century ago—industrializing young nations undergoing rapid urbanization—bears little resemblance to today's world of postindustrial globalization, superdiversity, and superinequality. What is certain is that we want more education than ever before. From poverty to inequality, from crime to incarceration, from global competition to sustainability, from health to well-being, in *la pensée Américaine*, education is the answer almost regardless of the question. We don't ask of medicine, engineering, or computer science what is routinely asked of education. With such great expectations, disappointments abound, especially when education's silver bullets go off target. Eternal ambivalence, it seems, has now taken center stage.

Alas, education can't do everything. But we have a better register of what it can do. The pathways by which education energizes fraternal and sororal bonds, accelerates status mobility, reproduces inequality are more clearly delineated data-wise and conceptually, even as they are vigorously debated. So are the relationships between education, health, and various human development indices. What has been needed for some time is broad *aggiornamento* on education's virtues qua democratic practice and citizenship. We need a reunion, a rendezvous, with Dewey and Durkheim but also with John Rawls and Hannah Arendt.

FROM CITIZENS TO CONSUMERS

With the ascendancy of economic scholarship, the language that has come to articulate disparate claims for education is replete with market ideas like "investments," "premiums," and "returns." The conceptual architecture that defined education scholarship and practice during the formative era— Durkheim's "conscience collective," Dewey's "social reconstruction"—evoke, if anything at all, a quaint bygone era. That edifice is a bit like historic Havana: a once magnificent architecture now faded, sad, irrelevant. We are in a world where the logic of the market is the hammer for the nail of all education's problems. Education is about efficiency, outcomes, and returns. Algorithmic metrics delineate pathways from teacher "inputs" to student "outcomes." The first principle—that "every dollar invested in education"[7] shall deliver results in the currency of better skills, better jobs, and better income—has penetrated shared cognitive schemas globally, over the loud protestations of reproduction theorists in the French-inspired Anglo-American traditions. Arguably no other idea has traveled as well, even across fiercely contested cultural and epistemic boundaries: from preschool to college, the new *mentalité* announces that education pays in little and big ways. In the words of

Nobel Laureate James Heckman, "the economic strength of any nation depends on the skills of its people."[8]

In this tradition, investments in education yield significant, even superb, returns. Advocates of sustainable development have come to sharply focus on the logic of investments in education moving forward. The eminent Columbia University economist Jeffrey Sachs writes, "Of all of the investments needed to achieve sustainable development, none is more important than a quality education for every child."[9] And in comparing the Chinese development strategy to his native India, another economist Nobel Laureate, Amartya Sen, has argued that the Chinese strategy of "expanding human capability, through education and healthcare" is perhaps responsible for cutting the deep poverty rate globally by half in just two generations.

Quality early childhood education has come into sharp focus as new cognitive neuroscience data suggest that early interventions, in the first thousand days of life, are best suited to reverse the ravages of poverty.[10] The "preschool pays" data come from James Heckman's classic studies of early childhood education. Heckman monetizes further returns, arguing that early childhood education may be the best palliative for the depredations of poverty: "Investing in quality early childhood development for disadvantaged children from birth through age 5 will help prevent these achievement deficits and produce better education, health, social and economic outcomes. Such investment will reduce the need for costly remediation and social spending while increasing the value, productivity and earning potential of individuals. In fact, every dollar invested in quality early childhood development for disadvantaged children produces a 7 percent to 10 percent return, per child, per year."[11] The logic of the market (an astronomical "7 percent to 10 percent return"), not the ethic of rights or the requirements of democracy, drive the argument.

At the other end of the education pipeline, economists are also busy making the case for college education with equal gusto. Even in the era of skyrocketing higher education costs, a college education produces, we are informed, superb returns. MIT's David Autor argues that with the "dramatic growth in the wage premium associated with higher education and cognitive ability," college now is better than free. He estimates that over the course of a lifetime, the cost of a college degree today is an amazing "negative

$500,000." Alas, according to the good economist, not going to college can cost you perhaps half a million dollars.[12] The *New York Times* headline says it all: "A Simple Equation: More Education = More Income."[13]

The nexus between education, the economy, and jobs consumes more and more space—a virtual data tsunami flooding the leading journals. In its vulgar form, the idea of education for jobs consumes all the oxygen— asphyxiating its eudaemonic, emancipatory, and democratic values. The faux pas over the so-called Wisconsin idea saw the sacrifice of the idea of education as a search for truth and a practice of freedom at the altar of education as a search for jobs. In February 2015, "Scott Walker, the governor of Wisconsin and potential Republican presidential candidate, unveiled a proposed budget that would cut $300 million of funds to the University of Wisconsin system and shift power over tuition from the Legislature to a new public authority controlled by appointed regents. The initial draft of Mr. Walker's budget bill also proposed to rewrite the university's 110-year-old mission statement, known as the Wisconsin Idea, deleting 'the search for truth' and replacing it with language about meeting 'the state's work-force needs.'"[14]

With globalization, inequality has been naturalized as the new normal. Sharp spikes in inequality have generated new lines of scholarly inquiry examining the relationships between education (operationalized as the distribution of skills, competencies, and sensibilities) and wealth. The French economist Thomas Piketty deploys vast historic and comparative data suggesting inter alia that inequality is poised to surpass previous historic records. As the returns to capital outpace the returns to labor, the accumulation of wealth via capital dwarfs gains in wages and labor. As inequality grows to Pharaonic proportions, education takes on a new democratic urgency.

In the United States, the data on inequality tell the sobering story of a tiny and shrinking share of the total population continuing to amass vast wealth. Credit Suisse reports in its 2014 Global Wealth Data Book that the "share of the top 10% . . . rose gently from 67% [of the wealth] in 1989 to 72% in 2007 and then jumped to 74.5% in 2010. Figures just released for 2013 indicate a further rise to 75.3%. These findings suggest an upward shift in wealth inequality in recent years." Worldwide, the wealthiest 1 percent now owns almost half the world's wealth: "[the top 0.7%] of adult population, own 44% of global wealth."[15]

Wealth and income disparities are linked to education from pre-K to college. Researchers in disparate fields—demography, psychology, sociology, anthropology, economics, and neuroscience—drawing on multiple methodologies have examined the links between parental socioeconomic standing and children's long-term outcomes. An abundance of data suggests that parental income, family structure, family size, mother's education, and father's participation in the labor market have strong effects on a child's development and education. The research shows that such parental factors have effects on multiple child outcomes, including literacy, completed years of schooling, socioeconomic mobility, physical and psychological health, as well as brain development. The range of effects, again, is detected in preschool and persists all the way to college. As early as ages two and three, children of disadvantaged parents are found to have lower cognitive skills as measured by standardized tests. The gap goes on all the way to college (Duncan 2014).

As the world becomes more unequal, the broad distribution of skills, competencies, and sensibilities can and should work to interrupt the intensification of economic disparities. In Thomas Piketty's words, "Historical experience suggests that the principal mechanism for convergence [of incomes] at the international as well as the domestic level is the diffusion of knowledge. In other words, the poor catch up with the rich to the extent that they achieve the same level of technological know-how, skill, and education."[16]

NOSTALGIC ABOUT THE FUTURE: SCHOOLING IN THE AGE OF SUPER DIVERSITY AND SUPER INEQUALITY

Worldwide, more children are in schools now than ever before[17] and even the most modest gains in schooling generate significant virtuous cycles over and beyond the now-privileged market-inspired metrics. Starting with the less obvious data on education, data on gender and health are both intriguing and confirm an old Darwinian hypothesis.[18] Robert LeVine and his colleagues at Harvard have shown how even marginal gains in early literacy among girls produce measurable intergenerational results in health and well-being in disparate contexts. With reading, they argue, children achieve mastery of the so-called academic and bureaucratic registries—language practices not found in the familial spaces of kin and kith but that are essential for navigating the impersonal world of institutions such as schools, bureaucracies, health clinics, and the like.

Women's schooling is strongly related to child survival and other outcomes beneficial to children throughout the developing world, but the reasons behind these statistical connections have been unclear. . . . Communicative change plays a key role: Girls acquire academic literacy skills, even in low-quality schools, which enable them, as mothers, to understand public health messages in the mass media and to navigate bureaucratic health services effectively, reducing risks to their children's health. With the acquisition of academic literacy, their health literacy and health navigation skills are enhanced, thereby reducing risks to children and altering interactions between mother and child. Assessments of these maternal skills in four diverse countries—Mexico, Nepal, Venezuela, and Zambia.[19]

At the base of Maslow's hierarchy of needs, what education does is saves lives.

In a nostalgic ethnography about the future, the developing world is reaching even more children, at earlier ages, with engaging programs for longer periods of time. Better infrastructures are getting children to safe schools. Information technologies are playing a muscular and innovative role: "The spread of computers, mobile phones, and broadband coverage to the poorest regions of the world could—and should—ensure that every child in low-income countries has access to the same trove of online information and quality learning materials as children in high-income countries."[20]

The world's high-income countries are also facing obstacles of Pharaonic dimensions to get to a nostalgic ethnography of the future. Allen's *aggiornamento* on the broad foundations of education is thus urgent and imperative. In the United States, we are witnessing the confluence of two formations: (1) mass migration's deep demographic echo (with children of immigrants now the fastest-growing sector of the child and youth population) and (2) growing levels of inequality naturalized as a new normal. US schools are now educating the most diverse cohort of young people since the advent of mass schooling over a century ago. The cohort of students that enrolled in American schools in the fall of 2014 is the first cohort of the new "minority-majority generation." Approximately one-quarter of all youth are of immigrant origin, and it is projected that by 2020, one in three of all children will be growing up in immigrant households.

In the United States, immigrant students arrive at school both healthier and more optimistic than comparable samples of nonimmigrants. They are also learning English faster than in previous waves of mass migration. Latino children are a case in point. The 17.5 million children and youth of Latino origin, two-thirds of them immigrants or the children of immigrants, are now America's largest and fastest growing ethnic minority group. A recent study by Child Trends reports the following:[21]

- In regard to important socioemotional skills, young Latino children enter school on a par with or even exceeding their non-Latino peers.
- The majority of Latino children live with two parents, which offers a firm foundation for emotional and economic well-being.
- More young Latino children are enrolling in early education programs. Latino students are posting solid gains on national assessments in key subject areas — putting aside here whether they are Allen's proper assessments. More Latinos than ever before have a high school diploma, and record numbers are enrolling in postsecondary education.
- Latino children are more likely than children in other racial/ethnic groups to eat dinner with their families six or seven nights a week.
- Hispanic teens match or even exceed their peers in other racial and ethnic groups in their avid use of technology.

According to a Pew Hispanic analysis, "76.3% of all Hispanics ages 18 to 24 had a high school diploma or a General Educational Development (GED) degree in 2011, up from 72.8% in 2010. And among these high school completers, a record share — nearly half (45.6%) — is enrolled in two-year or four-year colleges." The report concludes, "Hispanics are (now) the largest minority group on the nation's college campuses, a milestone first achieved last year."[22]

There is a lot to celebrate, but as Quiara Alegría Hudes notes in her commentary, our *alegría* (joy) is interrupted by real sorrows. For too many immigrants, schools lead to dystopia, not utopia. We can say that Latinos arrive in the United States with an *educación* advantage[23] — the socioemotional and other health and psychological advantages in the Child Trends data, but leave our school with an educational disadvantage. Rumbaut writes, "An important finding supporting our earlier reported research is the negative association of length of residence in the United States with both GPA and aspirations. Time in the United States is, as expected, strongly predictive of improved English reading skills; but despite that seeming advantage, longer residence in the United States and second generation status [that is, being born in the United States] are connected to declining academic achievement and aspirations, net of other factors."[24]

In a different voice, Reverend Virgil Elizondo, rector of the San Fernando Cathedral in San Antonio, Texas, articulates this same problem: "I can tell by looking in their eyes how long they've been here. They come sparkling with hope, and the first generation finds hope rewarded. Their children's eyes no longer sparkle."[25] New immigrants know that they must learn to navigate the rough waters of schools in the new society. But growing inequality proves to be a powerful undertow threatening to drown immigrants, reverse mobility in subsequent generations, rupture the fabric of the immigrant family, and make the democratic promise an elusive mirage for our newest Americans.

The children of immigrants have "greater market-income poverty rates than children in native-born families."[26] For them there is more, not less, inequality: in 1999, 22.8 percent of Latino children were living in poverty, compared with 7.7 percent of whites.[27] In 2006, however, the poverty rate for Latino children had nearly doubled that of Caucasian native-born children (28 percent and 16 percent, respectively). For immigrant Latino families, poverty rates reach higher percentages, with 35 percent of foreign-born Latino immigrants living in poverty, compared with 27 percent of their second- or third-generation counterparts.[28]

Inequality's radioactivity is hidden in plain sight. In the United States, children of immigrants are four times as likely as native-born children to live in crowded housing conditions and three times as likely to be uninsured, and 39 percent of Latino immigrant families report difficulties affording food.[29] Children raised in poverty are vulnerable to an array of distresses, including difficulties concentrating and sleeping, anxiety, and depression, as well as heightened exposure to delinquency and violence. Poverty has long been recognized as a significant risk factor for poor educational outcomes.[30]

Poverty coexists with a variety of other factors that augment risks such as single parenthood, residence in violence-ridden neighborhoods, gang activity, and drug trade, as well as school environments that are segregated, overcrowded, understaffed, and poorly funded. Poverty, however, is not solely an inner-city phenomenon: today, more of those residents live in suburbs than in big cities or rural communities, a significant shift compared to 2000, when the urban poor still outnumbered suburban residents living in poverty.[31] Poverty is also associated with high rates of housing mobility and concurrent school transitions that can be highly disruptive to educational performance.

Immigrant origin Latino children are the most segregated students in US schools. Segregation coupled with poverty matters, Orfield and Lee argue: "The high level of poverty among children, together with many housing policies and practices which excludes poor people from most communities, mean that students in inner city schools face isolation not only from the white community but also from middle class schools. Minority children are far more likely than whites to grow up in persistent poverty. Since few whites have direct experience with concentrated poverty schools, it is very important to examine research about its effects."[32] Immigrants who settle in predominantly minority neighborhoods may have little, if any, direct, continuous, and intimate contact with peers from the nonimmigrant mainstream population. A pattern of triple segregation—by race, language, and poverty—shapes the lives of many new immigrants in varied countries.

Poverty and segregation are often compounded by unauthorized status. The United Nations estimates that there are between forty and fifty million unauthorized migrants worldwide. The United States has the largest concentration of undocumented immigrants in the world: approximately eleven million people are unauthorized. There are approximately 1.1 million youth living in the United States without proper documentation, and millions more are living in households headed by at least one undocumented immigrant.[33] Research suggests that since undocumented youth often arrive after multiple family separations and traumatic border crossings,[34] they may continue to experience fear and anxiety about being apprehended, separated again from their parents, and deported.[35]

A large proportion of undocumented workers are employed in low-paying professions with erratic working conditions. Unauthorized migrants do not access social services that could serve to mitigate the harshest conditions of their poverty.[36] Psychological and emotional duress takes a toll on the experiences of youth raised in the shadow of the law, which has also been documented through narrative and qualitative research.[37]

Protracted poverty, deep segregation, and unauthorized status are the ingredients for dystopia and alienated belonging of the second generation in many immigrant-impacted societies. In the United States, large and growing numbers of poor immigrants of color and the undocumented are de facto relegated to spaces where the socially constructed phenotype aligns with entrenched patterns of segregation and marginalization of native minorities. Portes and Zhou have appropriately termed this dynamic as "segmented assimilation," wherein certain immigrants join the marginalized space of native minorities, creating what they term a new "rainbow underclass."[38]

EDUCATION'S UNHAPPY FAMILIES[39]

US education lamentations revolve around the twin poles of mourning the past and outright panic about the future. The structure of our discontent has diachronic and synchronic vectors. In the master narrative, we are doing worse than before (the diachronic vector), and at the same time, we are falling behind others (the synchronic vector).

Once the envy of the world, we are now seemingly failing in measure after measure, from preschool to college. If we are our age's Rome, American education has become an empire of mediocrity. Without going into the rabbit hole of imperfect measures and assessments that Allen examines in chapter 1, the data add up to a dystopic story.

Whereas 81 percent of children in the developed world enrolled in preschool last year, only 69 percent were enrolled in the United States. Whereas two generations ago our country led the world in the percentage of high school graduates, today we are at a mediocre eleventh place. Recent Organization for Economic Cooperation and Development (OECD) data suggest that among newborns to twenty-five-year-olds, we now rank an abysmal twenty-third in the estimates of youth and emerging adults who will complete high school over their lifetime. In Los Angeles, the nation's second largest unified school district, only 64 percent of the class of 2014 seems to be on track for graduation—failing miserably according to one of Allen's yardsticks. Two generations ago, we ranked third in the world in college graduation rates, but comparative OECD data show that fewer than 50 percent of American twenty-five- to thirty-four-year-olds have completed college. While 31 percent of college students drop out in the world's high-income countries, in the United States, over 50 percent will drop out. A 2014 article by Eduardo Porter indicates that barely 30 percent of American adults have achieved a higher level of education than their parents did. . . . In Finland more than 50 percent of adults are more educated than their parents. And matters are getting worse, not better. Among 25- to 34-year olds, only 20 percent of men and 27 percent of women . . . have achieved a higher level of education than their parents. It's even bleaker at the bottom: Only one in 20 Americans aged 25 to 34 whose parents didn't finish high school has a college degree. The average across 20 rich countries in the O.E.C.D. analysis is almost one in four.[40]

Our failings with regard to the eudaemonistic qualities of education are recognized by some, but not as many as Allen would like. The antonym of eudaemonia reigns in the American classroom. Many years ago, we did a simple experiment asking students to complete the sentence, "School is _____." Tallying the replies to the sentence-completion task, we got to a crux of education and the antonym of eudaemonia. The overwhelming answer was "boring."[41]

If schools are falling short on animating education's eudaemonic impulses, we seem to fall short at citizenship, too. Scholars and concerned observers alike deplore education's rachitic preparation of youth for the most elemental requirements of citizenship, such as voting, serving in a jury, understanding law making, and such—a topic carefully examined by William Damon and his colleagues at Stanford.[42] But today, most of the lamentation centers on education's failure to cultivate the cognitive and metacognitive skills and the socioemotional grit said to be required to function in a workforce under the regime of globalization.

Our unhappiness vis-à-vis eudaemonia, citizenship, and the labor market of the twenty-first century betrays a metapreoccupation: Just how are we to reimagine American education for the new era of globalization?

It is in the context of this new metapreoccupation that Allen's claims are most important. The tour de force archaeology of the vocational and liberal approaches to education—with brief detours peeking into the "scribal training centers in ancient Egypt and the ancient Near East and philosophical, rhetorical, and medical schools, as well as early schools for children in Greece and Rome" and then the universities of Bologna, Paris, and Oxford—reminds us of education's origins in structures and ambitions that are allocthonous to our current preoccupations. In nation building, Allen suggests, there are transformational moments when customary practice becomes metabolized into legitimate and codified bureaucratic practice. In Allen's words, the "moment when legitimate public officials acquire authority for a practice that has previously been managed mostly by private individuals, as for instance when a society gives up allowing individuals to effect retribution for wrongdoing . . . and instead designates public authorities to manage responses to wrongdoing."

Turning then to cultivate education's terrain, Allen gets to work using Rawlsian tools from his "Two Concepts of Rules." Rawls's classic distinction, we are reminded, hopes to differentiate the general claims for justifying an institution or practice versus justifications for the actions undertaken within such institutions. First order claims in education (i.e., when the state sets the structures for mass public schooling) tend to follow a syntagmatic narrative structure, while the justificatory claims of the second order follow a more paradigmatic narrative logic. In the syntagmatic narrative, claims tend toward the utilitarian: the state is in the business of setting schools in the service of the economy, citizenship, security, and such. The second order claims, centered on what happens in the quotidian rhythms of schools, follow a more strictly paradigmatic logic where utilitarian and humanistic claims contain each other in varied states of equilibrium and disequilibrium.

The sharp binary divide in education between utilitarian claims versus eudaemonistic claims is thus recast by Allen into more fluid states of co-construction. Before turning to her "humanistic baseline" for education, Allen brings to the table someone seldom invited to education soirées: Hanna Arendt of *The Human Condition*. In Allen's gaze, the elemental structures of Arendt's normative ideal for a humane condition offer a conceptual way forward. In Arendt's architecture, the preparation of every soul for the human condition entails readiness for "(1) breadwinning work, (2) civic and political engagement, (3) creative self-expression and world making, [and] (4) rewarding relationships in spaces of intimacy and leisure." These structures are constituted by complex molecules originating in both the instrumental (or utilitarian) and expressive (or humanistic) sides of the periodic table of elements. With regard to breadwinning work and civic and political engagement, Allen finds the individual and state aims of education coming together—even with interruptions in the easy flow between the individual and the state. In the twenty-first century, these interruptions increasingly in-volve cultural contestations.

If the conceptual "cleaning up" Allen performs in these pages is admi-rable, I ask for more. In our longing for the future, we need an education for a decidedly post-Herderian world that is at once ever more interconnected and interdependent but also more divided and fragile—the world of glob-alization. Granted, as Allen argues, "as a consequence of the relatively late arrival in Western history of education as a fully autonomous sociopolitical practice on a par with punishment, economics, and war, scholars are still in the early stages of coming to understand its logic." But such punting is not so well justified as Zhou Enlai's supposed answer to Richard Nixon's ques-tion about what he thought of the 1968 cultural revolution: "It's too soon to tell." It is not too soon to tell that the logic of education needs a fundamental recalibration to the logic of globalization. It is not too soon to tell that glob-alization has shaken the foundations upon which Rawls builds the first order claims that are essential for Allen's claims.

Globalization is the most disruptive force in education in a hundred years. Globalization's three Ms—"markets," their integration and disintegration; "migration," the mass movement of people on a planetary scale; and "media," the new communication, information, and social media technologies—challenge the deep structures of the nation-state and interrupt the taken-for-granted Herderian ideals and longings for alignment and coherence with regard to language, identity, region, and *das Volksgeist*. These ideals, deep in the mitochondrial DNA of the Prussian education systems we inherited, are made increasingly anachronistic by globalization.

In an earlier cycle of globalization and mass migration, we erected the as-similationist structures of the public education system to turn illiterate Euro-pean peasants into loyal citizens and productive workers of young, confident, and ever-more-muscular new nations. Glocalization, the midpoint between globalization and localization, announces a post-Westphalian moment where the nation-state's existential *raison d'être*—vis-à-vis war, the economy and society, and yes education—is beginning to resemble the drunk who lost his keys at a dark bar but is looking for them on the street corner under the lamp where the light is.

Children growing up in today's America are more likely than in any pre-vious generation to face a life of working and networking, loving and living, flourishing and communing with others from different national, linguistic, religious, and racial backgrounds. They need the skills, competencies, and sensibilities to be prepared, borrowing another of Allen's ideas, for what it takes to authentically "talk to strangers." But they are also growing up in a new normal of massive inequalities where they are at once closer to and more distant from those "strangers." The ethos and the eidos of the institutions changed, with their formation deformed by a triumphalist market logic orthogonal to Aristotle's eudaemonic flourishing, to Arendt's requirements for citizenship and the human condition, to an ethic of rights, or to the elemental requirements of Durkheim's social cohesion. Scholars, policy makers, and engaged citizens clamoring to hit education's reset button to start the hard work of charting a new path for education in a new era will find in Allen's "humanistic baseline" an elegant, rational, and humane map. Those who take the longer view will rejoice in this overdue reunion.

"Participatory Readiness" and the Courts
Michael Rebell

The theme I will pursue in my commentary is the role that courts can play in implementing the important concept of "participatory readiness" that Danielle Allen has articulated. Preparing students to function as capable citizens in a democratic society, the aim of participatory readiness, has historically been a major goal of public education. In recent years, a series of state court cases involving students' right to an adequate education has revived and given constitutional prominence to this goal. Neither state legislatures nor education officials have, however, followed through in actually implementing these decisions, nor so far have the courts seriously enforced them. Allen's insightful explication of what civic preparedness means can help motivate and give them the tools to now do so.

To understand the prevailing trend in contemporary educational expectations, let me begin by discussing the Common Core State Standards that have been adopted by more than forty of the states and the "college and career readiness" objective toward which these standards are directed. These standards and this objective, though not free from controversy, are the latest development in the standards-based reform movement that has been the predominant thrust of education reform in the United States for the past twenty-five years.

Standards-based reform originated in the 1980s in response to the *Nation at Risk* report[1] and a growing sentiment that the United States was in danger of falling behind other countries in the international economic competition, largely because of our students' mediocre academic performance. In 1989, President George H. W. Bush convened a national education summit, attended by all fifty governors and many corporate CEOs, to deal with this perceived education crisis. A commitment to adopt challenging academic content and expectations in all our nation's schools emerged from this meeting. With strong federal encouragement, almost all the states developed and adopted standards in each of the core academic subject areas, and many of them then began to reform their education systems to train teachers and to develop curricula and accountability systems geared to these standards in an attempt to ensure that all students would meet the standards. The No Child Left Behind Act, enacted by Congress in 2002 with strong bipartisan support, was designed to provide some financial support and enforcement rigor to bolster these state actions. The adoption of Common Core State Standards with "college and career readiness" as the ultimate goal is a further enhancement of standards-based reform that many states have now adopted.

Implicit in standards-based reform and in the college and career readiness goal is an expectation that our education systems can achieve both equity and excellence. In other words, the current education policy of both the federal government and nearly all the states has been built on an assumption that virtually *all* students can perform at very high levels and can meet challenging graduation requirements. This expectation is consistent with America's historic democratic assumption that all citizens have the capacity to vote intelligently and to participate in other forms civic engagement. However, as Allen has pointed out with reference to the writings of Michael Schudson,[2] the concept of citizenship and the definition of who is included in that category have changed dramatically over time. The radical expansion of the concept of citizenship in our day to include formerly excluded minorities, women, people from low-income backgrounds, and an overall highly diverse population has rendered the need to educate all students for democratic participation both more significant—and more difficult to achieve.

The joint pursuit of both equity and excellence is an inspiring motif that has stimulated major efforts to overcome educational inequities and has raised expectations as to what all students actually can achieve, whatever their racial, ethnic, or class background. In contrast to past practices that tracked students into either "vocational" or "college preparation" programs, current "college- and career-ready" standards assume that all students should pursue a similar, rigorous educational path and that all of them are capable of meeting virtually the same challenging graduation requirements. The reality is, however, that although we have made some progress toward meeting these goals, in 2014, the year in which the drafters of the No Child Left Behind law had expected—and, indeed, mandated—that 100 percent of American students would be meeting challenging state standards, we are, in fact, far from achieving these aims. For example, on the latest National

Assessment of Education Progress, only 35 percent of the nation's eighth graders were proficient in mathematics and only 36 percent in reading.[3]

Accordingly, many educators and policy makers are now rethinking the directions that state legislatures, education officials, and schools need to take to achieve equity and excellence. Some are wondering whether in recent years there has been too much emphasis on measuring outcomes, particularly on student performance on standardized tests in a few subject areas, and too little attention paid to the inputs—investment in teaching and learning and the resources, services, and supports needed to provide effective programs to all students. For this more expansive understanding of what students' need for school success, Allen's discussion of "participatory readiness" is particularly timely and important.

As noted above, standards-based reform had emerged from concerns about the ability of American students to compete in the global marketplace, and strikingly little attention was paid to the other prime goal of education—that is, preparing them for capable citizenship. Allen has now appropriately rekindled interest in the importance of educating all students in the humanities in general and in education for democracy in particular. Her exposition of participatory readiness should inspire policy makers and educators to ensure that students are not only "college and career ready" but "college, career, and *citizenship* ready."

Although educators and policy makers have been neglecting the importance of educating students for civic participation in recent times, the courts have not. Judges' involvement in this conversation about the goals of public education may surprise some people who assume that the courts do not weigh in on education policy matters. The fact is that sometimes they do. In recent years, many state courts have given particular attention to the purposes of public education and, in doing so, have consistently emphasized the importance of preparing students to be capable citizens.[4]

This interesting turn of events has occurred in the fiscal equity and education adequacy cases that have been filed in forty-five of the fifty states since 1973. In that year, the US Supreme Court held in *San Antonio Independent School District v. Rodriguez*[5] that education was not a "fundamental interest" under the federal constitution. This ruling closed the doors of the federal courthouses to litigants seeking to ensure adequate funding for schools in

low-income and minority school districts in order to rectify historical patterns of underfunding for their schools. The decision left it solely to the state
courts to consider these claims. Under most state constitutions, education
is considered a "fundamental interest." Although the state courts historically had not been aggressive in dealing with civil rights issues, in this area,
the state courts proved responsive. Plaintiffs prevailed in the first state court
cases brought after the *Rodriguez* ruling, and that led other advocates to file
cases in almost all the other states. Overall, plaintiffs have won over 60 percent of these cases.

Initially, the state education finance cases focused on the denial of "equal
protection of the laws" to the poor and minority students who attended
school in underfunded districts. More recently, however, these cases have
been based on clauses in virtually all the state constitutions that can be
read to guarantee students an "adequate" education. The language differs
from state to state: in New York, students are entitled to the opportunity to
a "sound basic education";[6] in New Jersey, "a thorough and efficient education";[7] in Washington, an "ample education";[8] and, in Florida, "a high quality
education."[9] But whatever the phrase, the underlying common theme is the
identification of some basic level of education to which every child is entitled.

In these cases, the state courts have demonstrated an insightful understanding of the standards-based reform approach. They have used state standards as guidelines for their constitutional analyses of the deficiencies in
current education financing systems. Essentially, the judges recognize that if
the state's policy is to hold all students to challenging educational standards,
then the state is responsible for providing all students sufficient resources to
have meaningful opportunities to meet those standards. In order to assess
the extent to which students are being denied such opportunities, many of
the courts have deemed it important to define a constitutionally adequate
education. In doing so, many of them have examined the intent of the drafters of the education clauses in their state constitutions — most of which were
written in the eighteenth and nineteenth centuries — and articulated in contemporary terms the purposes of an "adequate" education.

In examining the original intent of the constitutional framers and relating
that intent to contemporary needs, these courts have uniformly emphasized that children are entitled to adequate educational opportunities that

will both prepare them for the competitive global marketplace and equip them to function as capable citizens in a democratic society. Interestingly, the courts have generally spoken first about preparation for citizenship before talking about economic competitiveness. For example, the New Jersey supreme court defined the constitutional requirement as "that educational opportunity which is needed in the contemporary setting to equip a child for his role as a citizen and as a competitor in the labor market";[10] the Texas court stated that the intent of framers was to diffuse knowledge "for the preservation of democracy . . . and for the growth of the economy";[11] the Wyoming supreme court defined the core constitutional requirement in terms of providing students with "a uniform opportunity to become equipped for their future roles as citizens, participants in the political system, and competitors both economically and intellectually";[12] and the Connecticut supreme court held that the constitution entitles "students to an education suitable to give [them] the opportunity to be responsible citizens able to participate fully in democratic institutions, such as jury service and voting . . . [and] prepared to progress to institutions of higher education, or to attain productive employment and otherwise contribute to the state's economy."[13]

An early decision of the Kentucky supreme court has been especially influential in this area. Its analysis has been followed by many other states' highest courts, including those in Massachusetts, New Hampshire, North Carolina, South Carolina, and West Virginia. The Kentucky court defined a constitutionally acceptable education as one that has as its goal the development in each and every child of the following seven capacities:[14]

1. Sufficient oral and written communication skills to enable students to function in a complex and rapidly changing civilization
2. Sufficient knowledge of economic, social, and political systems to enable the student to make informed choices
3. Sufficient understanding of governmental processes to enable the student to understand the issues that affect his or her community, state, and nation
4. Sufficient self-knowledge and knowledge of his or her mental and physical wellness
5. Sufficient grounding in the arts to enable each student to appreciate his or her cultural and historical heritage

6. Sufficient training or preparation for advanced training in either academic or vocational fields so as to enable each child to choose and pursue their life's work intelligently

7. Sufficient levels of academic or vocational skills to enable public school students to compete favorably with their counterparts in surrounding states, in academics, or in the job market

These constitutional definitions line up quite well with Allen's delineation of the "vocational" and "humanistic" purposes of education and particularly with her detailed description of the need of society and of the individual for education to be preparation for "breadwinning work," "civic and political engagement," and personal "flourishing."

In her second chapter, Allen explicated with some particularity how education can and should relate to preparing students for civic and political engagement (and to some extent for personal flourishing) through her concept of "participatory readiness." Participatory readiness for Allen means providing students "verbal empowerment" and "democratic knowledge," which includes "bridging" and "bonding" skills and "tactical and strategic understanding of the mechanics of political action." The New York courts in the Campaign for Fiscal Equity (CFE) litigation,[15] in which I was co-counsel for the plaintiffs, also discussed in some detail the particular skills that students would need to function productively as civic participants. I will turn now to their discussion of the civic engagement theme and how it relates to Allen's concept of participatory readiness. I will then conclude with some thoughts about how Allen's perspective might encourage increased judicial enforcement of the civic engagement component of the right to a sound basic education and might thereby cause the states to take more seriously their constitutional obligation to implement participatory readiness.

In the first round of the CFE litigation, the court of appeals, New York's highest court, denied the state's motion to dismiss the case and sent it back to the lower court for a trial that, among other things, was to determine what exactly is the "sound basic education" to which all students are entitled. The court of appeals had preliminarily stated that "sound basic education" had as its purpose providing students the skills they need to "function productively as civic participants capable of voting and serving on a jury," but the court did not claim to know exactly what this meant; it instructed the trial court to hear evidence and to determine with more particularity what skills students would need to be effective civic participants.

At this point, our legal team was still a bit baffled with trying to determine what evidence we could use to identify the skills students would need to be capable civic participants. Fortunately, the trial judge came to our rescue. The trial had commenced in late October 1999. Two weeks later, there was a recess for Election Day. The next day, before the first witness was called, Justice Leland DeGrasse called all the lawyers up to the bench and, with a wry little smile, said, in essence,

> I was thinking about this case when I was voting yesterday. The court
> of appeals said that we should determine the skills students need to
> be voters. What I'd like you to do, therefore, is to have your education
> experts examine the proposition on restructuring parts of city
> government that was on the ballot yesterday in New York City and tell
> me whether the graduates of the city's high schools can understand that
> document. And, while you're at it, I want you also to take some of the
> documents that are being submitted to the jury in the case going on in
> the next courtroom and have your witnesses tell me whether the city's
> graduates can understand those documents.

So we now had a path forward for marshalling evidence to demonstrate the real-world skills students needed to be capable voters and jurors.

The main legal controversy between the parties in the CFE case was whether the constitutional right to a sound basic education should be pegged to a minimal sixth- to eighth-grade functioning level or to the challenging twelfth-grade functioning level reflected in the regents' learning standards that the state had recently adopted. The plaintiffs' witnesses graphically demonstrated, through slides displayed on courtroom screens, the relationship between the specific skills that students would need to comprehend particular sentences and phrases in the ballot proposition and juror documents and the knowledge and skills that were encompassed in the regents' learning standards.

First, these witnesses identified the specific reading and verbal skills that an individual would need in order to comprehend the meaning of various parts of the ballot proposition. They then discussed the "democratic knowl-edge" that students would need to understand the context of the changes in governmental structures that were the subject of the ballot proposition. Next, they focused on the particular English language arts, social studies, mathe-matics, and science concepts in the regents' standards that related to the ability to fully understand these complex documents. For example, they de-scribed the verbal and analytic skills a juror would need to comprehend and apply concepts like "the preponderance of the evidence," and they explained how other skills jurors might need, such as the ability to analyze statistical tables and graphs and to understand economic concepts like "opportunity costs," are developed through the mathematics, science, and social studies standards.

The defendants countered by introducing polling data showing that the vast majority of American voters obtain their information from radio and television news and make up their minds on how to vote for candidates and propositions before they enter the voting booth. The implied premise of the defendants' position was that citizens do not actually need to function at a high level of skill and that they need not be capable of comprehending com-plex written material, so long as the subjects dealt with in the material are regularly discussed in the mass media. The defendants also claimed that dia-logue among members of the jury could substitute for a lack of understand-ing of particular points by some of the individual jurors, thereby suggesting that all citizens do not need high-level cognitive skills and deep democratic knowledge, so long as they can obtain assistance from other citizens in carry-ing out their civic responsibilities.

Justice DeGrasse's decision resoundingly rejected this position:

> An engaged, capable voter needs the intellectual tools to evaluate
> complex issues, such as campaign finance reform, tax policy, and global
> warming, to name only a few. Ballot propositions in New York City, such
> as the charter reform proposal that was on the ballot in November 1999,
> can require a close reading and a familiarity with the structure of local
> government.
>   Similarly, a capable and productive citizen doesn't simply show up
> for jury service. Rather she is capable of serving impartially on trials that
> may require learning unfamiliar facts and concepts and new ways to

communicate and reach decisions with her fellow jurors. To be sure, the jury is in some respects an anti-elitist institution where life experience and practical intelligence can be more important than formal education. Nonetheless, jurors may be called on to decide complex matters that require the verbal, reasoning, math, science, and socialization skills that should be imparted in public schools. Jurors today must determine questions of fact concerning DNA evidence, statistical analyses, and convoluted financial fraud, to name only three topics.[16]

Although society may have unreflectively accepted a wide gap between its democratic ideal and the actual functioning level of its citizens in the past, now that the issue has come to the fore, it is difficult to conceive of any judge specifically endorsing, and our society knowingly perpetuating, a state of affairs in which voters cannot comprehend the ballot materials about which they are voting and jurors cannot understand legal instructions or major evidentiary submissions in the cases they are deciding. In order to function productively in today's complex world, citizens need a broad range of cognitive skills that will allow them to function capably and knowledgeably, not only as voters and jurors, but also in petitioning their representatives, asserting their rights as individuals, advocating for their communities, and otherwise taking part in the broad range of interchanges and relationships involved in the concept of civic engagement.

Much of Justice DeGrasse's thinking, as set forth in the lengthy quotation I just cited, clearly is consistent with the specific components of "participatory readiness" that Allen has developed. For example, the judge emphasized the considerable "verbal skills," the first element of participatory readiness, that future voters and jurors will need to develop in order to understand complex ballot propositions and jury documents. He also emphasized that to carry out these civic functions, they would need deep "democratic knowledge," as Allen puts it, in the form of "familiarity with the structure of local government."

The judge also specified that, in relation to "verbal skills" and "democratic knowledge," schools need to impart "verbal, reasoning, math, [and] science" at a sophisticated level because "jurors today must determine questions of fact concerning DNA evidence, statistical analyses, and convoluted financial fraud." The court also spoke of "socialization" skills, which imply the kind of "bridging and bonding" and "tactical political knowledge" that Allen has highlighted.

In essence, there is an implicit dialogue between Allen and the CFE court in describing the specific skills that students need to be able to function as capable civic participants in the twenty-first century. This is not surprising. Philosophers and courts have something in common that politicians and many policy makers lack: they both adhere to professional traditions of closely analyzing words and concepts and of constructing positions in relation to a knowledge base that the profession has carefully developed over the years in accordance with established norms. Neither philosophers nor judges deal in sound bites; they share a professional commitment to fully explain and justify all their statements in accordance with established standards and procedures.

I have been both surprised and disappointed that despite the prominence that the state courts around the country have given to the importance of educating students for civic participation, there has been little positive response from education officials or the schools and little follow-up monitoring by the courts. On the contrary, among the first programs and activities to be eliminated or curtailed by schools when funding was reduced in the wake of the recent recession were music and art classes, drama productions, school newspapers, model UNs, debate clubs, team sports, field trips, and other hands-on and service-learning opportunities. These are precisely the types of "bonding and bridging" activities in which students need to engage if they are to learn the socialization skills and the "tactical political knowledge" that they need to be capable civic participants.

Nevertheless, I do gain a renewed sense of optimism from the beginning of an implicit dialogue between Allen's concepts of "participatory readiness" and the position of the state courts in the education adequacy cases. There is potential synergy here that could lead to a more expansive conversation involving not only political theorists and courts but also policy makers and educators that could further develop the important concepts of participatory readiness and lead to their implementation in the public schools. The courts need the philosophical support and practical concepts that Allen has developed if they are to be more assertive in enforcing the civic participation requirements of a sound basic education. Similarly, Allen and other political theorists who are concerned about these issues need the authority of the courts to impress upon policy makers and educators the primacy of the civic preparation mission of the schools.

How might this dialogue between political theorists and courts develop in the future? Clearly that is a question that one cannot answer with any degree of certainty. Publication and broad dissemination of Allen's framework for participatory readiness is an important first step and can contribute to this dissemination process.

And I also think that lawyers like myself who believe in the importance of preparing students for civic engagement have an obligation not only to bring these ideas to the courts but also to suggest specific actions that judges can take to implement them. For example, plaintiffs in education adequacy litigations might ask courts to require states and school districts to do the following:

1. Delineate the range of content knowledge of government, economics, science, and so on and the verbal, cognitive, and associational skills that students will need to be effective citizens.
2. Provide students suitable and sufficient opportunities to develop civic engagement skills through participation in extracurricular activities, student government, local civic projects, or service activities and guarantee that these activities cannot be eliminated or curtailed because of recessions or other fiscal exigencies.
3. Ensure that schools appropriately teach values of tolerance and democratic deliberation.
4. Develop skills in students that will allow them to maximize the positive potential of digital and social media for promoting civic engagement.

In this realm, of course, a separation of powers between courts and the other branches of government has to be respected. Courts cannot and should not get involved in the details of educational policy making. It would not be appropriate for them to spell out the specific content of a social studies curriculum or to tell the schools precisely what extracurricular or active engagement and service learning activities they need to undertake. But courts can establish constitutional parameters to ensure that the legislative and executive branches carry out their constitutional responsibilities in these areas; they can insist these policy makers develop, implement, and maintain the particular policies and practices that will, in fact, prepare students for civic participation. Allen's powerful concepts of participatory readiness provide a valuable vocabulary and rich conceptual source for courts, legislatures, school officials, and educators to draw upon in carrying out these functions and in furthering their own important dialogue in this critical area.

A World of Cousins
Quiara Alegría Hudes

These essays have given me much to grapple with in my own thinking about how I teach and why, how we teach and why, and how I write and why. One notion strikes me in particular. What Danielle Allen evocatively dubs "verbal empowerment" hits home on a personal level, making me reflect back on my family experiences in the Puerto Rican community of North Philadelphia. This reflection involves both affection and fury, as I remember growing and developing a worldview and aesthetic in response to witnessing the "verbal disempowerment" of many of those I loved. Allen's concept of "verbal empowerment" also stirs me on a professional level, as a playwright and playwriting teacher.

In my comment, I'll apply some of my professional knowledge to Allen's arguments, introducing some of my field's vocabulary, discussing particular dramatists' approach to language, and anecdotally bringing up a few of my own instances of teaching. I will then use my family memories from North Philly as a kind of applied case study or litmus test toward some of Allen's arguments regarding equality.

While my discussion of pedagogy and drama will involve dispassionate consideration, my reflection on "verbal empowerment" as it relates to family will contain my deepest, most personal wishes for how we ought to educate.

Let me begin with three notes from my field.

Playwriting, and the study of playwriting, is one sliver of the humanities pie. Stanford University's own language describes the humanities as "the study of how people process and document the human experience." Indeed, when I teach playwriting to Philadelphia public school students or Wesleyan undergrads, reading great drama is at the core of our investigation. Great dramatists have processed and documented the human experience for the stage, and we study it. Even though my expertise represents a sliver of the humanities, I find there to be a few reverberations.

DEFAMILIARIZATION

Paula Vogel was my teacher at Brown University, where I received an MFA in playwriting. She is revered in the field for her decades of intrepid, ebullient teaching that nurtured an entire generation of playwrights—authors like Nilo Cruz, Lynn Nottage, and Sarah Ruhl. I am most lucky to be part of such a robust lineage, and indeed Vogel's pedagogy embraced teaching playwriting not only as a preprofessional endeavor but more deeply as an investigation of life itself, a way of thinking and living in the world, and an ongoing attempt to articulate the mysterious stirrings of the heart and vexing doings of society. Vogel was a humanistic teacher. Time and again, while breaking bread, drinking Ouzo, or sitting in a black box theater waiting for the house lights to dim, Vogel hammered home this notion that art should make us notice, should make what's familiar to us strange. (She encountered this concept in Viktor Shklovsky's Russian formalist literary theory.)

Vogel sometimes used a metaphor of getting ready for work in the morning. How many times have we driven to the office and gone, "Wait, did I unplug the iron? Did I turn off the coffee maker? Did I leave the keys in the door?" Or, for subway commuters, how many times have we arrived at our station unable to remember having transferred between lines or having swiped our fare card half an hour earlier? The morning commute, Vogel said, is a series of steps we automatize and therefore forget. We run on autopilot, proceed as though sleepwalking. The stage, Vogel offers, is a platform where the familiar is made strange again. The stage startles us out of our sleepwalking.

Extrapolate outward to the other tasks of our day: dusting, ironing, showering, eating, reading news, walking, loving. The more these tasks become automatized, the less it seems that our day has existed at all. Have we lived if we don't particularly remember the living? Are we in this world if we don't notice that we are? Shklovsky asserts, "Art exists that one may recover the sensation of life."[1]

I don't think the arts are singular in their capacity to wake us up. Language as a study and practice, "the interpretive and expressive skills" that Allen references, the deep investigation of how to listen and articulate, giving voice where there has been silence, also helps us "recover the sensation of life." I recall a simple phrase: "I have a dream."

Don't we all? Literally. Humans dream every night. We savvies often roll our eyes when people recount their dreams in self-indulgent detail, and yet King's phrase startles us back into an experience that connects us all and therefore implicates us all: "I have a dream."

Shklovsky challenges us to remember "holding a pen or . . . speaking a foreign language for the first time" and compare that with our feeling "at performing the action for the ten thousandth time. . . . Such habituation," he tells us, "explains the principles by which, in ordinary speech, we leave phrases unfinished and words half-expressed."[2] I would add that such habituation explains how in ordinary experience we leave questions unanswered or, more fundamentally, unasked.

There is something particular about the investigation of the humanities that challenges students to articulate—and therefore notice—our habitual actions, our automatized routines, our unasked questions. There is a close, dangerous relationship between our society's habitual behaviors and our society's habitual inequality. Inequality, in its various guises, becomes another morning commute: automatic, unremarkable. "Verbal empowerment" is a profound tool to make us notice the habitualized inequalities we participate in daily. In this particular way, the defamiliarization that verbal empowerment arms us with is a pedagogical pathway in support of equality.

VERBAL EMPOWERMENT AS EXPLORED BY TWO PLAYWRIGHTS

As Allen evocatively points out by quoting the ancient Greek rhetorician Gorgias, there is a "powerful, invisible body of language which dwells inside each of us." I believe the act of articulation is one of the beautiful treasures of this life. I use the word *articulation* with my students a lot.

Playwrights are finely attuned to the stakes of verbal empowerment, how its presence or absence can elucidate the inner worlds of their characters. One of the first questions a dramatist asks as a play world unfolds in her heart and mind is how the characters will speak. Aggressively? Rhythmically? Chaotically? Softly?

The Cuban American playwright Nilo Cruz makes a strong choice in his 2004 Pulitzer-winning drama *Anna in the Tropics*.[3] Cruz puts his fresh-off-the-boat Cuban immigrant characters—he actually dramatizes one of them arriving on a cruiser from Cuba—in a working-class cigar factory in southern Florida in the twenties. Rolling cigars is monotonous labor class drudgery, and yet Cruz renders these factory laborers stunningly eloquent. They speak in imaginative metaphors to explain their contrasting points of view to one another. Their speech is so lyrical and articulate that conflict becomes almost impossible; the eloquence of each character renders her point of view valid to the others, even when in opposition. These characters face very real challenges—the advent of cigar-rolling machines replacing the need for human labor, the subsequent demise of the "lector" as a person who reads literature aloud to the factory workers, and—in a bit of classical dramaturgy—a gun that will be fired by the end of the play. But, within this contentious environment, Cruz's characters come to an understanding rather than fighting. Their eloquence allows them love and community.

By contrast, I point to the work of contemporary German playwright Franz Xavier Kroetz, who was at his height of creative output in the seventies and eighties. Kroetz felt that language was a class problem. He focused his hefty oeuvre (thirty plays and counting) on working class characters, much like Cruz. But unlike Cruz, Kroetz's characters lack the skill to even partially express themselves, and so they suffer from and perpetuate their own alienation, loneliness, and rage. Kroetz developed an aesthetic around broken, impoverished speech. The results are often hideous to the point of comical. As critic Frank Rich said in a 1984 *New York Times* review, Kroetz's work "is not pleasant, but it sticks like a splinter in the mind."[4]

The play Rich was describing is Kroetz's grotesque romance *Through the Leaves*.[5] In it, a female butcher begins dating a brutish abusive laborer. To mark the new relationship, she begins to keep a diary. She might not have the verbal acuity to defend herself when her lover hurls insults her way, but what's truly disturbing is that even in her own diary, her expressive speech is so stunted that she seems to be writing herself out of existence. She wanted the diary, she chose the diary, but her desire doesn't give her the ability to actually articulate what it feels like to live in her skin.

I think these examples give us two vivid, if anecdotal, perspectives on how "verbal empowerment," even within the same social class, can have different outcomes on "human flourishing," to use Allen's phrase. Without language, Kroetz's characters wither. With language, Cruz's characters love and form community. They are Arendtian world builders.

SOME PERSONAL INSTANCES OF TEACHING

As a playwright, I am often asked, "Have you written anything I've heard of?" My answer? "Well, it's the theater, so most likely, no." As a playwriting teacher I am often asked, "Can you really teach someone how to write a play?" There is a suspicion of teaching playwriting held by many I speak to, a suspicion that I would posit extends to a widespread skepticism of the humanities as indulgent and soft or, more extremely, as untrustworthy and dangerous.

How do I justify teaching the class I teach—playwriting workshop—sometimes twice to the same student? Is my goal that students become professional playwrights with pieces on Broadway? Or is it "a flourishing life"? For me, it is the latter, and my experience tells me that playwriting is a rigorous and rich building block toward an "Arendtian life of action."

When I enter the classroom or sit at my writing desk, I think about technique and art a lot. Technique *and* art? Technique *versus* art? They're inseparable and yet often at odds. As I grappled with Allen's argument, I began to think that my technique/art dichotomy is not dissimilar from Allen's marketplace readiness/participatory readiness paradigm.

As a dramatist, I engage craft to articulate my ideas, to build tension as a story unfolds, to land a joke, to create climax and surprise. The building blocks of craft are teachable. They're quantifiable. In class, I urge my students to read deeply and closely—when does a playwright begin and end scenes and to what effect? How does a playwright use components of language—meter, repetition, punctuation, grammar, rhyme—to build a dramatic world? One student of mine recently observed that in the play *Ruined*, about civil war in the Democratic Republic of Congo, playwright Lynn Nottage ends almost every scene at its height of conflict, never allowing for a sense of resolution or rest until the final scene, which concludes with a gesture of comfort. A shrewd observation on craft. Another student noticed that in the dysfunctional domestic melodrama *August: Osage County*, Tracy Letts uses overlapping conversations to create a cacophony, building tension toward the explosive dinner scene, which is the fulcrum of act 2.

This is as close as I get to STEM. It's the mechanics and math of how dramatists make dramas. In this way, I do partially train students to be employed by HBO or Disney Theatricals or to enter a staff writing room at AMC and create engaging, entertaining, and sophisticated content. The anvil and hammer of scene craft, the asymmetry of character motivation—these tools help a playwright articulate her themes, ideas, and exploration of humanity. And yet a curriculum that focuses exclusively on craft misses the mark, errs on the side of shallowness, and doesn't necessarily produce great writers or plays. In fact, experience tells me it produces a collection of well-crafted but wan writing.

Before technique is even engaged, how does a playwright have an idea in the first place? How does she determine whether it's a fecund seed or a passing fancy? What elements of life are worth engaging onstage and memorializing on our library shelves? And once technique is engaged, how does a playwright tease out, wrestle with, and nourish her seedling of an idea so that it might become a bamboo patch or a redwood? And since ideas can be dramatized in myriad ways, *how* should she dramatize a given subject and why?

You can no more tell a student how to have an idea, or what idea to have, than you can tell her with whom she should fall in love, or how she should behave once in love, or whether it's love at all. And yet, thought is a practice—rigorous, engaged, challenging, rewarding—fundamental not just to drama but to science and math and democracy. Thought is a dynamic way of life, not a static deliverable lesson plan. In playwriting, we use words like theme and subject, but you can't dictate these things to students, and in fact, my own experience shows me that you can't even talk to students too directly or at too great of length about a theme or subject once they've chosen it. As Vogel teaches, "If you stare directly into the sun, you go blind." Instead, I see what my student is writing and give her a list: "Here are five masterful plays that have touched on your themes and subjects. Here's how a Russian formalist handled that topic. Here's how a German expressionist wrestled that theme. Here's how a Southern gothic danced with that notion. Now go read them closely, attentively, and bring me a new draft of your play that shows a dynamic response."

I've come to think that my role as a playwriting teacher is to create a dynamic laboratory for inward defamiliarization and outward articulation. If thought and articulation are muscles that get stronger with experience, then I want my laboratory to give students maximum opportunities to flex their interpretive and expressive muscles over time. When I first began my graduate studies in playwriting, I had a romantic notion of life as a writer but quickly became overwhelmed by the sheer volume of creative output that was expected. I asked Vogel, "But how can I have that many thoughts? How can I fill hundreds of pages with engaged expression?" "It's a muscle," Vogel winked. "It gets stronger." And it wasn't a muscle she could strengthen for me; I had to do my own heavy lifting within the dynamic laboratory she created.

NOTES FROM MY FAMILY

As I transition into talking about my family, I'd like to posit one microdefinition of equality: that a community's story, as told from within that community, be included in the recorded course of human events. This is the kind of equality I'm most concerned with in my daily practice, essentially—bearing witness to an American story that has not been brought to light as a part of who we are. This "cultural records equality" falls under the umbrella of political equality but also stands as its own thing. It is the charge my mother gave me when she urged me to become a writer.

My mother and stepfather hail from Puerto Rico and arrived in Philadelphia as young people who were shaky, at best, in spoken English. My maternal grandmother, a farmer, had made it through the second grade in Lares, Puerto Rico. My stepfather, an entrepreneur, never quite finished high school in Philly, though he came close and did graduate from the Job Corps. And my mother, an activist and spiritual leader, graduated high school and managed a few credits at the Community College of Philadelphia.

Growing up, I had this increasing dread that some of my closest aunts and cousins were invisible. The Puerto Rican neighborhood where they lived was isolated from the rest of Philly. Some fell prey to the AIDS epidemic in its early stages; others fell prey to the crack cocaine tsunami that submerged entire city blocks, and I have more than once witnessed the professional men in our family turn the ignition and begin the long journey to visit their sons in jail. I remember when a particular cousin, who had graduated from the Philadelphia public school system, admitted to me that she was illiterate. "How did you graduate?" I asked her. "They just pass you," she shrugged. "I just stood in the back." I remember another cousin who had graduated high school. When faced with a street sign or written instructions, she would ask me to do the reading, though she never straight up said she was illiterate and I never dared ask.

Another anecdote. A distant cousin, Tico, came from P.R. to Philly when I was in middle school. He moved in with us as a starting point and became my after-school babysitter. He had a spark and wit and energy that lit up my afternoons. He broke the unspoken law of nature that a human be defined as *someone who drinks cafe con leche every morning* because the young man awoke with tons of energy without any caffeine. But just as suddenly as he came into our home, Tico disappeared. Without a word or a trace, one afternoon he just wasn't there. Months later, my mom heard through the grapevine that Tico had run off to New York, where he would die swiftly, and alone, from AIDS. He disappeared rather than come out in our machismo community as a gay man who had contracted HIV.

Another anecdote, and this one cuts most closely to the bone. In 2009, I drove to Philly to interview a cousin about addiction and recovery, which she had experienced firsthand. I had always admired her ability, in a drug-addled neighborhood, to walk the mundane unglamorous path of sobriety, and I wanted to write about it. I remember her cupboards being relatively bare, but she offered me the last egg in her kitchen and fried it up with pride. I didn't dare refuse her gesture—"that's how we roll, Quiqui," she smiled. She spoke to me of the boredom and depression that drove her to addiction, and the quotidian commitment that had earned her twenty years clean. I enjoyed hearing her story, and she enjoyed being heard. After telling me particularly salacious stories, she'd say, "You gotta put that in your play, Quiqui." But our interview was cut short by police sirens. Two of my younger cousins, who lived across the street, were being arrested. I was like, "You have got to be kidding! Is the universe playing some sick joke on us?" As one particular cousin was loaded into the paddy wagon, he glanced up and caught my eye. There I was—Quiara, the one who got out, the one who stands tall, the anointed, the learned. And there he was, the psychologically troubled but sweet young jokester with whom I had broken bread so many times after school at Abuela's house, in cuffs. He returned his gaze to the sidewalk, was loaded into the paddy wagon, and it pulled away. Silence. A somber air now filled my cousin's living room. In fact, the young man with whom I had made eye contact was the son of the cousin I had been interviewing. "I'm sorry, Quiqui, can we finish the interview some other time?" she asked.

Three years later, I was wrapping up a session of advanced playwriting at Wesleyan. I turned on my phone and twenty voice mails chimed in quick succession. *Water by the Spoonful*, the play I wrote based on that interview, had won the Pulitzer in drama. As I drove home to New York that evening,

I recalled that visit to North Philly—an interview that remained unfinished, a little cousin still behind bars.

If all that was unexpected, what came next was a bizarre gift—a manila envelope from an upstate prison. My little cousin had written his first novel while incarcerated. It was hard to read—the spelling and handwriting were often illegible, and his pencil strokes had already faded significantly. Much of what I read was boring or random, but some of it had a spark—that glimmer or scream that excites us when we encounter a student's work or a new voice. My cousin *knew*. He knew of the "powerful, invisible body of language" dwelling inside him.

Allen tells us that "those with more sophisticated verbal skills are more ready to be civic and political participators." My young cousin remains unready. He's since been released and rearrested. He's about as far from "the levers of change" as one can get.

And yet he *knew*.

My deeply personal wish is for a humanities education that would teach my cousins to notice their automatized lives, to pay attention to that which has become so obvious as to seem unchangeable and inevitable, and to write it down: the poverty that they sleepwalk through every day, the policing, the jail time in relation to the alleged crimes committed, the crumbling health centers, the schools with padlocked libraries due to budget cuts, how we actually kill each other when we say "that shirt is gay," the schools with food stuck on the floors because custodial staff require salaries, block upon block upon block without a municipal trash can, the sidewalk as dumpster, how it feels to sit at the table of selfhood with these things as your daily bread.

I want them to notice, too, the pockets of their lives where vibrancy lives and breathes, though these things may also seem so obvious as to be unremarkable: the oral histories passed through generations; the recipes of poor elders that nurture an impressive amount of bellies; the gift culture where neighbors informally provide daycare and food services to each other in times of sickness; the willingness to risk imprisonment by joining a community in unapologetic protest (my family is virtuosic in the art of protest); the generations upon generations who have served in our armed conflicts; how Abuela once told me, "If you can't afford baby powder, put some corn starch on the baby's butt"; the notion that humility is the highest virtue; the reverence for community members who are *servicial*, of service; the knowledge of how a Yoruba *bata* becomes an Afro-Caribbean congo, becomes the clave beat, becomes an ass moving across a dance floor. Our *educacion*.

Yes, my deeply personal wish is that my cousins walk into their local schools and begin to see their barrio with defamiliarized eyes so that their mundane is rendered remarkable, in their own words—that their stories become part of the recorded "course of human events" our Declaration of Independence charges us to pay attention to.

In the task of having my cousins articulate what life in *el barrio* is, there is an implicit truth, which is this: El barrio is not a given. El barrio does not go without saying. It is not gravity. It is not a law of nature. It is a description of now. Tell us how things are today, thus allowing the possibility that they might be different tomorrow. This articulation, this noticing and describing, does not necessarily constitute civic participation, but it does at the very least mean throwing one's hat in the ring; it means anteing into the game of our democracy.

Allen asserts that "the critical question for a democratic society is how we can bond with those who are like us so as to help us bridge even with those who are different from us." I believe that when a critical mass of our truths are articulated other groups may have their senses shaken. Other groups may begin to notice, may find themselves defamiliarized. "Oh, they're a part of our world, too? They bring these gifts to the table, and they demand these considerations? Oh, let us take notice. They are a part of our morning commute."

I want my cousins to have jobs, yes, absolutely, but I have a deeper ambition for them, one that includes and eclipses the marketplace: that my cousins not just be world inheritors but also become world builders.

Response to Commentators
Danielle Allen

In my two chapters, I sought to identify some features of practices of education, as human beings have developed them historically and over time, that might tell us something about what is shared by the cluster of phenomena that the term "education" identifies for us. I have focused on those contexts—Ancient Mediterranean, European, English—that have most immediately flowed into the traditions out of which US educational institutions emerged. In other words, I identified a set of practices that bear a family resemblance to one another and then tried to say something about that family resemblance. Moreover, I focused on the practices of a subset of the world's cultural traditions, although with a bit of a comparative eye to the differences between the European and other traditions. I noted, for instance, that Chinese traditions of education were formalized far earlier than in the Western context. My method, in other words, is pragmatist, not metaphysical, more Deweyan or Wittgenstinian than Platonist—more about that pragmatism anon and more, too, anon, about other traditions and globalization, which Marcelo Suárez-Orozco has asked me to attend to more carefully.

The purpose of identifying a core to education—established over time through practice—is to ascertain whether there is any intrinsic connection between it and equality. I argued that there is, in particular in the connection between education and the empowerment of people as political agents. The political competitiveness that has historically flowed from education is itself a force for egalitarian reforms in other domains, most importantly the economic and the social. Ensuring that education continues to provide resources for political competitiveness requires, I argued, focusing on the "humanistic baseline" generally, regardless of what subject areas are at the center of a student's work. Preserving this element of education also necessitates deploying the humanities, specifically, to help develop "participatory readiness" in all students.

By way of identifying a family resemblance among different forms of schooling, I picked out their orientation toward the development of human

[99

capacities. In his acute comment, Tommie Shelby suggests that I might instead have picked out learning through formal instruction. Shelby also argues that I should have picked out "knowledge" and the "pleasures of contemplation," rather than "skill," as the relevant outcomes for the work of education. Thus, to give more detail to my portrait of the family resemblances that give content to the term "education," I need to do a better job of explaining what I mean by "human capacities."

Based on my argument, a reader could determine that human capacities consist of those components of human functioning that permit us to labor effectively; politick efficaciously and judiciously; love wisely and in a way that is fulfilling; and praise, play, and celebrate meaningfully. But meaningfully to whom, you might ask? And fulfilling for whom? Meaningfully and in a way that is fulfilling to ourselves as we ourselves judge, I would answer. But this is not enough of an answer to the question that Shelby has raised about just what I mean by the development of human capacities and whether my meaning closes down human possibilities around a single conception of the good or provides liberal protections for the diversity of conceptions of the good that populate our worlds. An adequate answer to the question of what I mean by "the development of human capacities" requires a deeper account of how terms like "capacity," "skill," "knowledge," and "participatory readiness" relate to one another in my argument. I will also attempt to build on Quiara Alegría Hudes's remarkable extension of my argument about language as the powerful and invisible body inside each of us.

Before I pick up each of these threads, however, let me also make note of the final challenge in front of me. Michael Rebell has brilliantly digested important legal advances in the field of educational law. He has detailed a shift of focus from the federal to the state courts in litigation strategy for educational equity cases. He has drawn our attention to the frequency with which state constitutions not only include a right to education but also tether that right to preparation for civic participation. Finally, he has highlighted an important need: as lawyers and judges work to make good on the state-level constitutional commitment to an education for participatory readiness, lawyers and judges would benefit from a more detailed understanding of the relationship between education and civic agency. In short, lawyers need scholars. Rebell generously suggests that they even need philosophers. But do they?

As Suárez-Orozco points out, whereas philosophy was a leading voice in conversations about education in the early twentieth century, philosophers ceded their place first to psychologists and more recently to economists. Do we really want philosophers back in the conversation about education? Shelby has suggested one reason we should be wary of inviting philosophers back. Philosophers have a tendency to make arguments about "the good," failing to respect the limits of liberalism that ring-fence the just society as a place populated by plural, cohabiting accounts of the good. Rebell suggests that philosophers can usefully contribute to the efforts of the courts to "establish constitutional parameters that ensure that the legislative and executive branches carry out their constitutional responsibilities in these areas [of educational policy making]." He commends my contributions in that direction. But Shelby worries that I have gone too far and have dangerously inserted a conception of the good into policy conversations. Have I in fact crossed the line drawn by liberalism to limit philosophy's contribution to public life? Or does my argument count as a restrained, nonimperial approach to philosophy that can make valuable contributions to public policy?

To answer these questions, I need to follow all the threads tagged here: the question of the basis on which I identify some feature of a cluster of practices all labeled "education" as giving "education" its core meaning; the question of what I actually mean by "the development of human capacities"; the problems introduced by my reliance on a "Western" tradition to identify the core feature of "education," especially in an era of globalization; and the question finally of whether philosophers can, in this wonderfully pluralistic age, usefully contribute to policy making. Finally, I will say one last word about education and equality.

PRAGMATISM

"Beliefs are rules for action," the late-nineteenth-century philosopher and psychologist William James famously wrote, thereby identifying an alternative framework for testing the content of ideas than, say, Platonic metaphysics had long seemed to provide. He meant that we can understand the content of an idea, a value, a normative claim only after we have begun to see how it affects the world. Once someone tries to act on the basis of a normative claim, what changes around them? What practical effects do their beliefs have? If new beliefs secure a better set of experiences for those impacted by the actions stemming from them, then those new beliefs are good.

But how are we to know whether the set of experiences emerging from the new ideas were "better" than the experiences the relevant group of people had previously? We have to count on those people to make judgments, based on conversation among themselves, about their own flourishing. Pragmatism, like Aristotelian eudaemonism, rests on the belief that human beings can fare better or worse; they can flourish or not. Aristotle sought a once-and-for-all account of that flourishing by studying nature. Pragmatists, in contrast, achieve accounts of flourishing through democratic means. Like John Stuart Mill, they recognize each individual as engaged in the business of determining whether he or she is happy.[1] They recognize that because none of us *can* know the minds of others, other than partially, hazily, and wishfully, none of us is in a position to make a sound determination of what will count as happiness for another.[2] Each of us must do that for ourselves. Understanding what counts as human flourishing therefore requires two things. First, it requires social forms that permit individualized explorations by each person of his or her own happiness. Second, it requires democratic conversations that permit the cohabitants of a community, of a nation, of the globe to seek solutions—for all decisions that we must necessarily make together—that best permit us to bring our multiple views about flourishing into alignment with one another. Democratic eudaemonism shares some features with Aristotelianism, but it is fundamentally pragmatist, rather than neo-Aristotelian, because on this account, the question of what makes us happy can be answered only through democratic means.

The second sentence of the Declaration of Independence provides a particularly profound statement of this pragmatist approach to democratic eudaemonism. Here it is in full:

We hold these truths to be self-evident, that all men are created equal, that they are endowed by their Creator with certain unalienable Rights, that among these are Life, Liberty and the pursuit of Happiness,— That to secure these rights, Governments are instituted among Men, deriving their just powers from the consent of the governed,—That whenever any Form of Government becomes destructive of these ends, it is the Right of the People to alter or to abolish it, and to institute new

Government, laying its foundation on such principles and organizing its powers in such form, as to them shall seem most likely to effect their Safety and Happiness.

The final clause is the most important for our purposes. From generation to generation, we must survey our circumstances, "the course of human events," and *judge* whether our government, whose purpose is to secure our rights to life, liberty, and an individualized pursuit of happiness, currently succeeds. Where it does not, we must revisit the basic terms of our social arrangements and reorganize them "as to us shall seem *most likely* to effect our Safety and Happiness" (emphasis added). The best we can do is make a probabilistic judgment about the joint structures that are "most likely" to achieve flourishing for all of us, a collective "safety and happiness." Moreover, we make this judgment, conceding our own fallibility as we make it. We know, as we act, as we do our best to judge rightly, that another generation will come along and correct us. The greatest philosophical contribution of the Declaration of Independence is its articulation of a species of pragmatism—this democratic eudaemonism.

Pragmatism works forward by helping us determine what to do. It gives us intellectual and normative tools for inching our way toward individual and collective flourishing. Yet pragmatism works backward, too. That is, we can use it to probe past historical practices for the values and normative commitments around which they were organized.

Let's return again to William James's idea that beliefs are rules for action. A feature of a rule is that if it is applied consistently over time, it generates patterned behavior. Over the last three decades, in the United States, the rule has been introduced that children must be buckled into car seats. The result of this rule is that families have, on the whole, needed bigger cars to accommodate multiple car seats for their children. The average size of American vehicles has therefore increased and, one speculates, American fuel consumption has, too, as a consequence of the rule about car seats. To find the logic in a set of practices, as I deploy that idea, is to seek out the beliefs that led to the habitual behaviors that give a practice its patterned look.

This approach to studying sociopolitical phenomena is also similar to Pierre Bourdieu's method in *Outline of a Theory of Practice*.[3] As Bourdieu analyzes practices, they are not stable, not static, as in a structuralist account.

Instead, any given actor faces a set of social rules and may or may not decide to deploy them, as they have been most recently used by those who preceded her on the stage. The rules are made and remade with these ongoing pragmatist reengagements with them. As the poet Frank Bidart writes, "We fill preexisting forms and when we fill them, we change them and are changed."[4] Rules can be remade and beliefs evolve along with them, but some social phenomena do nonetheless coalesce with more durable rules. State formation is a type of human development that has effected a near freezing into place of some norms—particularly those that pertain to marriage, markets and property, war and punishment, and (the latecomer) education. I had a twofold goal in excavating the "logic" of education and trying to make us aware of how long-standing customary "rules of action" define it. First, I wanted to ascertain where those rules for action represent things that we too value and perhaps need to work harder to protect. Second, I wanted to identify where those rules represent beliefs that we might want to shift.

Among the beliefs that I see operating in practices typically identified as examples of education is the idea that teachers and students interact to develop the student's human capacities and do so because this development is positively valued. In truth, I don't see a great difference between "capacity development" and "learning," nor do I see a great divide among the terms "skills," "knowledge," and "capacities." I had best explain why not. In my attempt to do so, however, I will trespass onto the territory that now belongs to psychologists. I am therefore likely to make significant blunders. Yet I am going to trespass nonetheless because I have been invited to do so, hoping only that this trespasser's blunders may perhaps provoke some novel lines of inquiry for psychologists.

A HUMANIST'S PSYCHOLOGY

I will make my argument without relying on experiments, survey work, or any other sort of statistical analysis. Instead, I will make my argument based only on an effort to scrutinize (a) my own experience as both teacher and student, (b) the experiences of my hundreds (but not thousands) of students, and (c) my conversations about teaching and learning with other teachers. Based on this body of experience, I draw inferences. I make judgments.

The mathematical methods developed in the middle of the twentieth century, first by statisticians and then by game theorists, and deployed so effectively by economists and now psychologists have displaced just this practice of judgment. Thus my purpose in trespassing on psychological turf is partly to make "judgment" as a practice visible again and to affirm its value, even while recognizing that judgment can be strengthened by assistance from the tools available to both experimental psychologists and economists. Yet while their statistical tools supply strength—defined as an increased likelihood of validity for claims—inferential judgment based on experience provides speed. Very often, when we need to make probabilistic judgments about what "shall seem most likely to effect our Safety and Happiness," we must do so before the psychologists and economists can complete all the relevant experiments and analyze all the available data. This is why the cultivation of sound inferential judgment from experience—the work, fundamentally, of the humanities—is so important. My accounts, then, of "skills," "knowledge," "capacities," and "learning" represent my best judgment, as of now, of the case.

I was surprised to find the concept of "skills" taking such a prominent place in Shelby's treatment of my argument. I had not thought that I had based my argument about education's purposes around that concept. Indeed, when I went back to look, I found that I had not directly included "skills" in my own writing in the first chapter. I had quoted many instances of contemporary public discourse that highlight "skills" as the main objective of education but in my own voice had argued only for "capacities." Yet in the second chapter, when I turned to focus on one of the specific capacities that I think education should foster—namely, "participatory readiness"—I did indeed then make an argument about the "skills" and "knowledge" that must be cultivated in order to foster the development of a capacity for civic agency in students. In other words, in my argument, "capacities" rest on "skills" and "knowledge."

Yet even this makes matters too simple—for "skill" is a very old word, coming, as one can hear, from Old Norse. Its earliest, if now obsolete, meanings are very capacious. The Oxford English Dictionary gives these early definitions:

a. Reason as a faculty of the mind; the power of discrimination
b. To have discrimination or knowledge, especially in a specified matter
c. That which is reasonable, proper, right, or just

The mystery of human intelligence is that "skill" and "knowledge" are not fundamentally separable, nor are "learning" and "capacities." While learning is pleasurable, and we can and should acknowledge that pleasure, I think it is impossible to learn without developing capacities of some kind. Nor can one "know" things or even enjoy the sheer joy of contemplation without "doing things": retrieving pieces of information from wherever they are stored in the brain, synthesizing and connecting, comparing, juxtaposing new things with one another, applying the knowledge to context, and so forth. Knowing depends on the same cognitive and metacognitive capacities that need to operate for "doing," understood as the deployment of "skills." Building up those underlying cognitive and metacognitive capacities helps both knowing and doing.

In ordinary language, we are far more comfortable talking about the body's well-being than about the mind's well-being. The body takes in food. The digestive system turns it into energy for immediate use but also into muscles, bone, hair, nails, blood, and so on, all the material stuff of life that permit us, physically, to go on. If we do right by our production of muscles, bone, blood, and so on over the long run, we get health, well-being, strength, beauty, and so on. Of course, these outcomes are not entirely in our control. The point is only that a commonsense understanding of physical health and well-being is readily accessible to all of us. As Marcelo Suárez-Orozco points out, it is possible to develop more sophisticated understandings of that physical well-being, and education often helps us acquire that.

But what about our brain and/or mind? What commonsense notions do we have about mental or intellectual well-being? Not many. Yet we can use the analogy of the physical body for thinking about this, too. Day in and day out, we take things into our mental apparatus—through perception and also through memory. Then with cognitive, metacognitive, affective (or emotional), and intersubjective (or relational) functions, we digest what we've taken in. Through that process of digestion, we may well experience pleasure—just as the body, thanks to digestion, feels a boost of energy. We may also acquire knowledge or stored information. But we also build muscles—intellectual muscles, among which are basic literacy, understanding, creativity, critical thinking, judgment, and communicative skill, but also personality muscles, among which we find grit, ambition, resilience, and so on. And just as doing right by our production of muscles, bone, blood, and so on gives health, physical well-being, strength, and beauty over the long term, so, in my argument, doing right by our production of literacy, understanding, creativity, critical thinking, judgment, communicative skill, and personality factors like grit and resilience equips us to flourish over the long term at work, in civic life, in our cultural communities, and in our intimate relationships.[5] Those muscles provide us with the capacities to meet the four human needs that I sketched in the first chapter.

In her comment, Quiara Alegría Hudes explores beautifully how thinking is a muscle: "When I first began my graduate studies in playwriting, I had a romantic notion of life as a writer but quickly became overwhelmed by the sheer volume of creative output that was expected. I asked Vogel, 'But how can I have that many thoughts? How can I fill hundreds of pages with engaged expression?' 'It's a muscle,' Vogel winked. 'It gets stronger.' And it wasn't a muscle she could strengthen for me; I had to do my own heavy lifting within the dynamic laboratory she created."

Hudes helps us see the value of developing these muscles not only for art but also for the artistry of social life by focusing on the work of two playwrights who depict verbal empowerment, on the one hand, and verbal disempowerment, on the other, in working-class contexts.

Nilo Cruz portrays Cuban American workers in a cigar factory. Hudes has this to say:

Rolling cigars is monotonous labor class drudgery, and yet Cruz renders these factory laborers stunningly eloquent. They speak in imaginative metaphors to explain their contrasting points of view to one another. Their speech is so lyrical and articulate that conflict becomes almost impossible; the eloquence of each character renders her point of view valid to the others, even when in opposition. These characters face very real challenges—the advent of cigar-rolling machines replacing the need for human labor, the subsequent demise of the "lector" as a person who reads literature aloud to the factory workers, and—in a bit of classical dramaturgy—a gun that will be fired by the end of the play. But, within this contentious environment, Cruz's characters come to an understanding rather than fighting. Their eloquence allows them love and community.

Here the empowerment pertains to both civic flourishing and the capacity to participate in communities of shared cultural meaning.

Hudes contrasts Cruz's characters, who have linguistic empowerment, with those of Franz Xavier Kroetz, a German playwright for whom "language was a class problem." She writes, "Kroetz's characters lack the skill to even partially express themselves, and so they suffer from and perpetuate their own alienation, loneliness, and rage. Kroetz developed an aesthetic around broken, impoverished speech." In one play, a female butcher keeps a diary to mark her new relationship with an abusive laborer. Hudes writes, "She might not have the verbal acuity to defend herself when her lover hurls insults her way, but what's truly disturbing is that even in her own diary her expressive speech is so stunted that she seems to be writing herself out of existence." This character's verbal disempowerment blocks her, specifically from flourishing in the realm of intimacy.

For the second chapter, I used as an epigraph a quotation from the ancient Greek rhetorician Gorgias. Let me repeat it here: "Speech is a great power, which achieves the most divine works by means of the smallest and least visible body." Language, or logos, is a great power housed somehow inside us in the smallest, most invisible body. It is, in other words, a most unusual kind of muscle. Gorgias contrasts its maximal power with the smallest of bodies. Although language, or logos, is so small as to be invisible, it is as powerful as a potentate. This is a way of conveying a principle of economy. Language does a lot with a little. The ratio of power to size is headed toward infinity.

Indeed, the central mystery of language's power lies precisely in its efficiency. Language is always working simultaneously at cognitive, affective (or emotional), and intersubjective (or relational) levels. Mastering language—and the traditions of literature, philosophy, art, and music that constitute the archive of language over human history—requires mastering all these domains. But it also requires mastering a remarkable process of judging which of the things that language can do are operative when and which should be applied when. This is what makes it so hard to pin the humanities down with metrics and rubrics. Language does too much all at once. The focused study of language—that is, of literature, art, philosophy, music, the textual remains of human history—develops students along so many dimensions simultaneously that efficient measurement is thwarted.

In the first chapter, I raised the topic of assessment in the context of K–12 education. I suggested we should take some steps back, via a reconsideration of the basic purpose of education, and then start anew our pursuit of appropriate means of holding schools and teachers accountable. The same might be said in the context of the effort to assess instruction in the humanities and liberal arts in the context of higher education. Noble efforts are under way — take, for instance, the Association of American Colleges and Universities' (AACU's) VALUE Rubric Development Project (http://www.aacu.org/value /rubrics). Over a two-year period, the AACU led the development of sixteen rubrics whose purpose is to provide "valid assessment of learning in undergraduate education." The rubrics provide modes of assessing learning outcomes like "inquiry and analysis," "critical thinking," "civic engagement — local and global," "ethical reasoning," "global learning," and so on. But you can tell from these labels already that the rubrics must overlap, and they do. Each is dense, and most overlap with others of the rubrics, as in table 3.

When one tries to pry apart, for formal assessment, all the cognitive, affective, and intersubjective muscles that serious engagement with language, through the study of the humanities, develops *simultaneously*, the result is baroque.

Just as our work on assessment and accountability in the K–12 context should start fresh from recognition of the two concepts of education (the macro state-level concept and the micro interactional concept), so too our efforts in higher education to assess the humanities should begin again, from recognition of the principle of economy. The value of the humanities is that they do so much *all at once*. This requires a different approach to assessment than has been developed for the STEM disciplines (science, technology, engineering, and mathematics) outside the humanities. They too may do a lot all at once, but that is ancillary, not central, to their purpose, at least as they are currently defined and taught.

A LIBERAL OR COMPREHENSIVE ACCOUNT OF THE GOOD?

I have argued, then, that by engaging with language generally and in the humanities specifically, we develop muscles, or capacities, on which our well-being depends. I have made an argument that the sort of well-being we should care about as we go about developing our intellectual and psychological muscles involves labor, civic action, cultural participation, and intimacy. My interest in the developmental role of intellectual engagement is neces-

TABLE 3. *Civic engagement: Local and global rubric*

This was one of sixteen rubrics developed by the Association of American Colleges & Universities to be used for assessment of undergraduate liberal arts education. The full set is available at https://www.aacu.org/value/rubrics.

	Capstone 4	Milestones 3	Milestones 2	Benchmark 1
Diversity of communities and cultures	Demonstrates evidence of adjustment in own attitudes and beliefs because of working within and learning from diversity of communities and cultures. Promotes others' engagement with diversity.	Reflects on how own attitudes and beliefs are different from those of other cultures and communities. Exhibits curiosity about what can be learned from diversity of communities and cultures.	Has awareness that one's own attitudes and beliefs are different from those of other cultures and communities. Exhibits little curiosity about what can be learned from diversity of communities and cultures.	Expresses attitudes and beliefs as an individual, from a one-sided view. Is indifferent or resistant to what can be learned from diversity of communities and cultures.
Analysis of knowledge	Connects and extends knowledge (facts, theories, etc.) from one's own academic study/field/discipline to civic engagement and to one's own participation in civic life, politics, and government.	Analyzes knowledge (facts, theories, etc.) from one's own academic study/field/discipline, making relevant connections to civic engagement and to one's own participation in civic life, politics, and government.	Begins to connect knowledge (facts, theories, etc.) from one's own academic study/field/discipline to civic engagement and to one's own participation in civic life, politics, and government.	Begins to identify knowledge (facts, theories, etc.) from one's own academic study/field/discipline that is relevant to civic engagement and to one's own participation in civic life, politics, and government.
Civic identity and commitment	Provides evidence of experience in civic-engagement activities and describes what she or he has learned about her- or himself as it relates to a reinforced and clarified sense of civic identity and continued commitment to public action.	Provides evidence of experience in civic-engagement activities and describes what she or he has learned about her- or himself as it relates to a growing sense of civic identity and commitment.	Evidence suggests involvement in civic-engagement activities is generated from expectations or course requirements rather than from a sense of civic identity.	Provides little evidence of her or his experience in civic-engagement activities and does not connect experiences to civic identity.

TABLE 3. *Continued*

	Capstone 4	Milestones 3	Milestones 2	Benchmark 1
Civic communication	Tailors communication strategies to effectively express, listen, and adapt to others to establish relationships to further civic action.	Effectively communicates in civic context, showing ability to do all the following: express, listen, and adapt ideas and messages based on others' perspectives.	Communicates in civic context, showing the ability to do more than one of the following: express, listen, and adapt ideas and messages based on others' perspectives.	Communicates in civic context, showing ability to do one of the following: express, listen to, and adapt ideas and messages based on others' perspectives.
Civic action and reflection	Demonstrates independent experience and shows initiative in team leadership of complex or multiple civic engagement activities, accompanied by reflective insights or analysis about the aims and accomplishments of one's actions.	Demonstrates independent experience and team leadership of civic action, with reflective insights or analysis about the aims and accomplishments of one's actions.	Has clearly participated in civically focused actions and begins to reflect or describe how these actions may benefit individual(s) or communities.	Has experimented with some civic activities but shows little internalized understanding of its aims or effects and little commitment to future action.
Civic context/ structures	Demonstrates ability and commitment to collaboratively work across and within community contexts and structures to achieve a civic aim.	Demonstrates ability and commitment to work actively within community contexts and structures to achieve a civic aim.	Demonstrates experience identifying intentional ways to participate in civic contexts and structures.	Experiments with civic contexts and structures and tries out a few to see what fits.

Civic engagement is "working to make a difference in the civic life of our communities and developing the combination of knowledge, skills, values, and motivations to make that difference. It means promoting the quality of life in a community, through both politic and nonpolitical processes" (excerpted from *Civic Responsibility and Higher Education*, edited by Thomas Ehrlich, published by Oryx Press, 2000, p. vi). In addition, civic engagement encompasses actions wherein individuals participate in activities of personal and public concern that are both individually life enriching and socially beneficial to the community. *Evaluators are encouraged to assign a zero to any work sample or collection of work that does not meet benchmark-level performance.*

sary, I would contend, because I think there is no such thing as learning or knowing without also building up one's intellectual muscles (or failing to do so), just as there is no eating and digesting that doesn't have an effect on the body's development. If, indeed, we can't learn, or know, or contemplate *without* developing "muscles" (or capacities), then surely one does want to attend to the direction of the development, if for no other reason than to strengthen the likelihood that one can deepen one's access to the pleasures of contemplation by developing ever-improving capacities for contemplation. That observation returns us to Shelby's questions about whether my account of the human capacities that ought to be fostered by education imports a conception of the good.

I will have to concede that, to some degree, my arguments about education *do* import a conception of the good. But liberalism, too, imports a conception of the good. There is no positive argument for how we should organize our common life that can avoid that. The relevant question, I think, is only whether the conception of the good argued for is liberal or comprehensive. I believe I have, in fact, put forward a liberal conception of the good, one that precisely makes room for plural conceptions of the good; that expressly seeks to combine *educación*, as Suárez-Orozco calls the diversity of cultural resources provided by family and kinship networks, with formal education; and that should even offer resources for responding to globalization. Let me explain. To do so, I will have to return to my conception of "the good," or rather of human flourishing, as I suggest in chapter 1.

We should enjoy learning, and a test of its success should be that it brings pleasure, not boredom, though surely it cannot bring pleasure exclusively, because learning is also often hard. Yet beyond what we gain in the moment of actual learning, we need to recognize the necessary developmental element of learning and consider which human needs most fundamentally require the support of the intentional development of our capacities. I proposed four and suggested that while the state might reasonably attend to two of those, it ought to leave space for schools, teachers, students, and families to steer their own course to attend to the other two. We need, I argued, to do the following:

1. Prepare ourselves for breadwinning work
2. Prepare ourselves for civic and political engagement

3. Prepare ourselves for creative self-expression and world making
4. Prepare ourselves for rewarding relationships in spaces of intimacy and leisure

The first two of those are reasonably seen as equally the concern of the state and the individual. The latter two, I argued, are the concern of the individual, to be treated with deference and restraint by the state. The argument I make for state deference goes beyond requiring that the state not seek to control those domains. It also requires that the state leave space in the school day for communities of school leaders, teachers, parents, and students to decide how best to support development along the third and fourth dimensions. Moreover, I suggest no content in the third and fourth domains for what constitutes good, successful, or fulfilling outcomes. These are precisely the domains in which the point of education is, above all, to prepare people to be judges of their own flourishing and to establish their own course—to find their own conceptions of the good, to build relationships around them, and to contribute to cultural communities of value to them on their basis.

But this does not mean that schools are irrelevant here. Can we learn from others in those domains of cultural production and intimacy? Of course we can. The idea that we all need to find our own conceptions of the good to frame our participation in worlds of culture and in intimate social relations does not mean that the work must be solitary. The suggestion is that communities of teachers and learners, and families who are at work on *educación*, should collaborate to ascertain just how to scaffold the development of their children toward success in these two domains. Schools *may* well wish to engage the development of their students in the domains of creative self-expression and preparation for rewarding relationships in spaces of intimacy. My argument is that the state should not direct the choices being made in this regard by schools. Nor should it consume so much of the time in the school day that school communities cannot use their schools for these purposes too. We should encourage diversity on this front. As Marcelo Suárez-Orozco points out, the subsequent challenge for schools, if they can be freed from excessive state constraint, would be to improve our capacity to build on the *educación* that occurs at home in support of the formal education that happens in school. An approach to schooling that acknowledges the importance of time in the school day for preparation for creative self-expression and world making (by which I mean contributing to the production of culture and preparation for fulfilling intimacy) and that protects that time from state control ought to be able to leverage the cultural diversity that globalization has offered to us as a stunning resource for collective, social learning.

A final word on the conception of human flourishing that I have articulated here. Shelby has expressed concern that any account of human needs that goes beyond survival and basic physical health is too prescriptive. I have indeed gone beyond that bare minimum. My picture of human flourishing includes not only survival and physical health but also political freedom or equality, creative self-expression or the participation in cultural communities, and personal intimacy. This articulation of core human needs is not novel. It tracks the argument of the United Nations' Declaration of Human Rights as well as the work of scholars like Amartya Sen. My route to the argument—through a pragmatist development of a concept of democratic eudaemonism—is different. But the picture of human needs lines up with familiar accounts provided by liberalism. The only feature of my account that is perhaps worth flagging is its emphasis on political equality, the right to participate as an equal in politics, as a basic need. This right has been less defended in the philosophical tradition than one might expect. Aristotle, for instance, recognized the need to participate in politics as a basic need for *some* people but not for all. The Declaration of Independence fudged the question. Although John Stuart Mill and Isaiah Berlin both saw individual personal development as a core need and liberal institutions as a mode of protecting that right, neither considered political equality fundamentally necessary as a protection for that right of personal development. Rather than requiring the freedom to participate for all, they asked only that governments, however organized, protect freedom "from interference."[6] Berlin, in fact, had real qualms about what he called "positive liberty"—the freedom to participate in politics. Only with figures like Hannah Arendt and Amartya Sen has political equality become considered a fundamental right for all people, one whose status is itself necessary to secure the other rights.[7] This is the view that I, too, take. We have to extend the account of basic human needs beyond bare survival and physical health to political equality, because it is the last that ensures people have the tools to secure the former. As Amartya Sen puts it, before India became a democracy, it suffered from famines routinely, but it has not suffered from a single famine since independence.

Have I gone beyond this consequentialist account of the usefulness of political equality to argue that it is a good in itself? Yes, I have. If we can agree that our bodies should flourish and that we need bare survival and physical health, perhaps we can agree that we need to secure the health of that very powerful, invisible body inside us—our capacity for language, or logos, or thought. That "muscle" has a status no less significant than any of our other muscles. And one of the things that muscle does most importantly is make judgments about whether things are going well or ill for us individually and collectively and set a course that will take us in better directions. That is the political muscle, and it feels good to use it. Human flourishing involves the health of this muscle, too. Such is my considered judgment, and I ask you to judge it in turn.

CODA

The topic of the relationship of education to equality has come to be closely connected to the problem of inheritance. The inheritance of wealth, cultural capital, and social contacts has powerful impacts on social, economic, and political structures. Education is rightly seen as among the most important antidotes to the social forces unleashed by starkly unequal patterns of inheritance.

In the United States of the founding era, the new nation did away with aristocratic titles as part of its founding. It also did away with the rule of inheritance by primogeniture (the whole of a father's estate to go to the first-born son). The goal was a "middling" economy that had a preponderance of "middle-class" households, rather than letting wealth accumulate and concentrate in the hands of a few.

We currently live in a world of income and wealth inequality vastly greater than what existed in the middle of the twentieth century. These inequalities translate into inequalities in cultural and social capital that themselves flow directly into educational outcomes. We are constantly at work, in our educational policy conversations, to ascertain how to reduce the power of inheritance. We wonder whether we should limit the ability of the wealthy to give money to their own children's public schools while other public schools languish without private philanthropy.[8] We stop and think twice about whether parents have a right to give their kids all that extra cultural capital by reading them an extra bedtime story.[9] We are concerned when charter schools are populated by children whose parents have made an extra effort to get them there.[10]

The problem of inheritance challenges our bedrock belief that all children should have an equal opportunity, which means an equal starting point in the race of life, in Lyndon Johnson's famous image. The facts of inheritance, as we now know them, mean such an equal starting point does not exist and is not likely to exist in the immediately foreseeable future.

There is, moreover, a challenging paradox here. This country has intervened fundamentally in how inheritance is handled—as with the eradication of the law of primogeniture. Yet we also very much want to encourage parents to direct their energies to the improvement of their children's lot. That is, we want parents to do what they can to see that their children have better educations than they themselves did. We will do damage to valuable social energies if we work too hard to make the effects of inheritance nugatory. While we ought to restore the inheritance tax, we should not, in other words, tackle the problem of inheritance at the point where the ambition to pass something on is doing its best work: inspiring parents to do the most they can for their children's education. What then can we do instead?

We need to restore an economy that results in a more middling distribution of income and wealth and that revives failing patterns of social mobility. This requires construction of policy frameworks that take apart segregation; that alter the current relationships among jobs, housing, and transportation; that reorganize funding at the municipal and county level; that strengthen wages for service workers and other working class roles; and that dispense with the illegal drug economy. But how can we get alternative policy frameworks? Only with a more competitive political system.

We can't educate our way out of the inheritance trap simply by trying to reduce the wage premium on expertise, nor should we try to restrain the ambition of parents to see that their children are well educated. If, however, we care about egalitarian economic and social outcomes, then we desperately need to educate a citizenry ready to participate maximally in our shared project of self-governance. In other words, caring about political equality should also advance work on the economic dimensions of equality, including the challenge of inherited opportunity.

NOTES

CHAPTER 1

1 See Gallup's poll on the most important problems faced in America: http://www.gallup .com/poll/1675/most-important-problem.aspx (accessed September 19, 2015). Education was last on the list of Americans' most important issues in the 1960s and 1970s. The topic began moving up the charts in 1980 and hit the first position in 2000 (according to McGuinn 2010). Its salience has declined since then (one can analyze trend lines on the Policy Agendas Project website at http://www.policyagendas.org/page /trend-analysis#), but it still makes Gallup's top ten list.

2 Piketty 2014, p. 71.

3 The politics of education have generated three different egalitarian ideals: equality of opportunity, equality of outcome, and adequacy. Allen and Reich (2013), particularly the chapters by Susana Loeb, Helen Ladd, Rob Reich, and Anna Marie Smith, discuss the strengths and weaknesses of these ideals.

4 Allen 2011.

5 Allen 2014b. Compare with Anderson 2010, Hayward 2013, and Rothstein 2013.

6 Allen 2011.

7 Allen 2013b.

8 Allen 2010.

9 Allen 2012a; 2013c.

10 There is the related problem to which Aristotle first called attention in the fourth century B.C.E. in book 5 of the *Nicomachean Ethics*: one also needs to distinguish between whether one has arithmetic or geometric equality in mind.

11 Piketty 2014, p. 71.

12 To understand what I meant by saying that a social practice has a logic, consider a game—say, chess. The structure of the board, the properties assigned to the pieces, and the goal of victory presumed to motivate the players constitute the "logic" of the game. Within that context, strategic principles guide play, and those principles make sense only within that context. In this sense, they are emergent from the "logic" or the underlying structure of the game of chess.

Now take a social institution—say, punishment. There too is a basic underlying structure: the designation by someone of a wrong done by somebody, a desire to somehow respond to that wrong, and a set of rules that determine what counts as an appropriate response, with those rules varying from society to society. Depending on how the underlying logic of punishment has evolved in any particular social context, different normative and strategic principles will flow from the practice and shape the actions of participants. Those principles will not *determine* the actions of participants. Some may break from the normative patterns and begin to lay down pathways to new social norms around which broad social practice will coalesce.

In sum, I am using logic to designate the pursuit of a conventional goal in the context of a set of social rules and roles (provided by norms and institutions); as people navigate that structure, they do so by responding to action-guiding strategic and ethical principles. The concept stems originally from French sociologist Pierre Bourdieu's concept of a "practice" in *Outline of a Theory of Practice* (1977).

13 On scribal schools, see Woods 2006. We learn about one ancient Greek school for children in Thucydides's *History of the Peloponnesian War* from the fifth century B.C.E.

14 Wei 2012.

15 Katz 1976.

16 Obama 2012.

17 Romney 2012.

18 National Governors' Association 2010, p. 1, emphasis in original.

19 US Department of Education 1983.

20 Committee on Prospering 2007, p. 30.

21 Obama 2013.

22 Menand 2010, p. 53. See also Gutmann 2015.

23 Indeed, several scholars and leaders in higher education have lately been seeking to achieve that. See Gutmann 2015; and Rose 2012.

24 Rawls 1955.

25 I am paraphrasing, not quoting, Rawls. Of course, Rawls excavates the common utilitarian justification for the basic structure of society in order to eventually replace a utilitarian justification at this level with his justification from "justice as fairness." I adopt his diagnosis of social facts on the ground that utilitarian arguments are commonly those being used at the macrolevel of justification, but I do so without moving from that view to an adoption of the theory of justice. I seek to develop my argument about political obligation instead from the content of moves inside the game—the microlevel.

26 In response to Rawls's argument about practices, the philosopher Stanley Cavell distinguishes two ways in which the label "practice" might be applied: "We may be conceiving of [a practice] either on a par with institutions like kinship systems, law and religion, institutions which distinguish societies from hives or galaxies, general dimensions in terms of which any community of human beings will be described; or we may be thinking of it as a *specific* institution, on a par with monogamy or monotheism or suttee or death by stoning, institutions in terms of which one society is distinguished from another society, or from the same society at an earlier stage" (Cavell 1999, pp. 299–300). Cavell rightly saw Rawls as concerned with the first category of "practice." I am also concerned with the first category.

27 Here, readers who know Rawls's argument will notice that I am limiting my use of it to *sociopolitical* practices, which have been co-opted by the state, and am not applying it to practices generally. I am arguing that when Rawls distinguishes between the justification for a practice as such and justification for actions undertaken within the practice, his distinction succeeds, really, only for *sociopolitical* practices, where the state has

co-opted some domain of human social activity. In such cases, two actors are relevant to understanding the practice: the state and particular individuals who carry out actions within the domain of the relevant practice. That Rawls's distinction between the two kinds of justification should map on to a distinction between two kinds of actors should come as no surprise. He draws readers' attention to the fact that utilitarianism, understood in its original formulation, concerned social institutions and was used primarily as a criterion for judging social institutions, not for guiding the actions of individuals (Rawls 1955, pp. 18–19 and pp. 18–19n21). Insofar as he makes space for utilitarianism at the level of justifying practices as such, he is recovering a bounded approach to utilitarianism as relevant mainly to the societal level. When Stanley Cavell criticizes Rawls's argument in "Two Concepts," he focuses on the case of promise keeping and acknowledges that Rawls's argument works better for punishment, where formal institutions have been set up (Cavell, 1999, pp. 299, 308). In other words, Cavell is implicitly noting that if Rawls's argument works, it works for sociopolitical practices.

28 Utility captures the satisfaction that agents take in particular outcomes. Here is one basic formulation: "What does it mean to say that agents are self-interested? It does not necessarily mean that they want to cause harm to each other, or even that they care only about themselves. Instead, it means that each agent has his own description of which states of the world he likes—which can include good things happening to other agents—and that he acts in an attempt to bring about these of the world. The dominant approach to modeling an agent's interests is *utility theory*. This theoretical approach quantifies an agent's degree of preference across a set of available alternatives, and describes how these preferences change when an agent faces uncertainty about which alternative he will receive. Specifically, a *utility function* is a mapping from states of the world to real numbers. These numbers are interpreted as measures of an agent's level of happiness in the given states" (Leyton-Brown and Shoham 2008, p. 1).

29 Rawlings 2015.

30 If the social justification for democracy is preservation of the state form, then educational systems should look different around the world accordingly, as the world continues to hold differences in regime type. On this line of argument, a single international standard for assessing education (such as the Programme for International Student Assessment [PISA] test) will be dangerous to any state whose state form is not adequately captured by that assessment instrument.

31 Ladd and Loeb 2013, p. 20.

32 This thought runs in the opposite direction from the line of argument that Rawls pulled out of his separation of the two levels of justification. His purpose in pulling apart justification for the rules of the game from justification for particular moves in the game was to establish a framework for a concerted challenge to the use of utilitarianism to justify the former.

33 For a particularly compelling account of how to understand Plato's arguments on this subject, see Lear 1992.

34 I call this a "democratic view of human nature" because it is implicit in the construc-

tion of democratic institutions that draw everyone into political life while also expecting them to be active in other domains.

35 Democratic politics is fundamentally a project of negotiating difference. (And this was always true, even in homogeneous communities; increased demographic diversity simply makes the centrality of plurality more obvious.) See Ober 2008 and Ober 2010. I owe my reading of Hannah Arendt, and particularly my understanding of the economic significance of the arguments in *The Human Condition* (1958), largely to Patchen Markell.

36 The philosophical practice of establishing, in essence, caste systems, where particular social tasks are assigned to particular social classes, appears in non-Western traditions as well. See, for instance, London 2011.

37 As stated previously, I owe my reading of Hannah Arendt to conversations with Patchen Markell and his book manuscript, *Politics Against Rule: Hannah Arendt and The Human Condition* (forthcoming). On stringent efforts to determine what is necessary given a nonexploitation criterion, see Cohen 2009.

38 Here it is worth noting that as of 2010, the current US presidential administration advocated replacing the cohort model with a growth model designed to track individual student progress. As of 2010, multiple states were also switching to a growth model for accountability. See Blank 2010: "States have increased interest in the use of growth models for school accountability. Growth models are based on tracking change in individual student achievement scores over multiple years. A total of 12 states are utilizing growth models that provide estimates of whether student achievement will meet Adequate Yearly Progress (AYP) state proficiency targets within three years. These models were designed to meet the requirements of the No Child Left Behind (NCLB) Act. In addition, 13 states have developed and implemented growth models as required by state policy; these models use different formulas to measure growth for students and schools. This paper is an overview and description of current state activities with growth models." To learn more about the growth model, please see more at the Council of Chief State School Officers' resource list: http://www.ccsso.org/Resources/Publications/State_Growth_Models_for_School_Accountability_Progress_on_Developing_and_Reporting_Measures_of_Student_Growth.html#sthash.ZOpCt9pl.dpuf. There does not appear to have been much change in this area.

39 One of my favorite examples here is the decision in the New York public school system to release high-performing schools from the requirement to have a quality review yearly. The result was that those schools recovered significant amounts of time for focusing on teaching and learning, whereas the lower performing schools, which continued with annual reviews, in effect suffered from a routine tax on the amount of time they could devote to instruction and its improvement. See Childress et al. 2011.

40 E-mail correspondence, August 13, 2010.

41 These measures have other problems too: measuring college completion is value neutral; it bypasses any assessment of the educational value of the particular college for the particular student. Also, the fact that college is clearly beneficial to many people does

not mean that everyone should go to college. These two problems can be addressed by broadening the amount of detail used in this basic college-completion portrait. One might break down completion rates for categories of college and one might supplement this by drawing on IRS data for occupational reports, six years out, for those who have not attended college. These are all data-intensive projects and suggest that these sorts of accountability measures should be developed and reported outside of schools, perhaps through regional assessment consortia, in order to avoid drawing the time of principals and teachers away from their core activities.

42 Allensworth et al. 2014.

43 Allensworth and Easton 2007. See also Allensworth and Easton 2005.

44 To this end, the CCSR disseminates its reports in "briefs" for parents, teachers, and students on how to make use of the CCSR indicators to support student achievement. See an example of a "parent brief" here: http://ccsr.uchicago.edu/publications/what -matters-staying-track-and-graduating-chicago-public-schools.

45 Darling-Hammond and Weingarten 2014.

46 On problems with grades as a measure of student performance, please see Suárez-Orozco and Suárez-Orozco 2013.

47 I've undertaken that challenge in the context of pedagogy in the humanities and liberal arts in the higher education and adult education space through a research project called the Humanities and Liberal Arts Assessment (HULA), which is now part of the Project Zero research group at Harvard's Graduate School of Education.

48 Childress et al. 2011, p. 93.

49 My description of the PAR process is a paraphrase of the account provided in Karp 2012.

50 Karp 2012, p. 48.

51 Ibid., p. 46.

52 Ibid., p. 49.

53 Winerip 2011.

CHAPTER 2

1 National Governors' Association 2010, p. 1.

2 Arendt 1958; Sen 1999; Ober 2007; Allen 2014b.

3 Quoted in Reich 2013.

4 Piketty 2014, 71.

5 Ibid., p. 481–83.

6 Ibid, p. 474.

7 Ibid, p. 307.

8 Goldin and Katz 2008.

9 Glaeser et al. 2006.

10 For a superbly insightful essay on social norms, their bases, and the potential for changing them, see Prentice 2012.

11 Acemoglu and Robinson 2015.

12 Ibid., p. 1.

13 Piketty 2014, p. 308.

14 Acemoglu and Robinson 2015, p. 1.

15 If it is indeed possible for an adequacy framework to reduce the positional aspects of the good of education, then "adequacy" rather than "equality" may actually be the right allocative solution to the distributive justice problem.

16 "Attainment" refers to the number of years of schooling; "achievement" refers to the level of growth achieved during those years of schooling as exhibited by test scores. While it is theoretically possible to equalize attainment, it is not theoretically possible to equalize achievement because of individual variation.

17 Evidence for this claim comes from five years of experience in the MacArthur Foundation research network on youth and participatory politics. The question of which word—"civic" or "political"—to use in discussions of how to educate students for public life returns with a strange insistence and without much prospect of resolution.

18 Alinsky 1971.

19 This was a conference panel entitled "From Participatory Culture to Political Participation" at the Futures of Entertainment 6 conference at MIT in Cambridge, Massachusetts, on November 9–10, 2012. The video of the panel lives here: http://techtv.mit .edu/collections/convergenceculture/videos/21729-foe6-from-participatory-culture -to-political-participation (accessed March 6, 2015).

20 Schudson 2003.

21 Schudson, in contrast, does identify a single model, which he calls the "monitorial" citizen. The "monitorial" citizen fulfills a watchdog function with regard to office holders.

22 I've pursued an effort to anatomize political speech across numerous publications, including *Talking to Strangers* (2004), *Why Plato Wrote* (2010), "Art of Association" (2012a), "Discourse Ethics for Divided Publics" (2014a), *Our Declaration* (2014b), and *From Voice to Influence* (2015).

23 The literature on deliberative democracy is relevant here. See, for instance, the work of Jürgen Habermas, Seyla Benhabib, and Amy Gutmann and Dennis Thompson.

24 For a treatment of King in this direction, see Shulman (2008). On frame shifting, see Woodly (2015).

25 Here there is a literature from the study of sports on the ethics of fair fighting that is relevant, as well as the professional ethics of fields like law and journalism.

26 Schudson (2003).

27 These terms were used at the "From Participatory Culture to Political Participation" panel noted previously.

28 See Gallup's polls on low approval ratings for Congress: http://www.gallup.com/poll /1600/congress-public.aspx (accessed March 16, 2015).

29 On the levers of change, see Allen 2015.

30 Allen 2014a.

31 Gardner 2015.

32 On the last point, see Mantena 2012.

33 For a particularly powerful treatment of the figure of the statesman, see Lane 1998.

34 Compare to Allen 2014b; see also McAfee 2015.

35 American Academy of Arts and Sciences 2013.

36 Ibid., p. 12.

37 Ibid., p. 24.

38 See Bennett, Wells, and Freelon 2009.

39 Here I effectively reproduce Aristotle's division of rhetoric into deliberative, forensic, and epideictic. The forensic (or judicial) aligns with my category of adversarial speech, and the epideictic, which involves pointing out what is noble and shameful, aligns with my category of the prophetic.

40 For a count of all the committee work involved in the production of the Declaration of Independence, see Allen 2014.

41 de Tocqueville 1990 [1835–40]; Putnam 2000. For a portrait of the alternative kinds of association being pursued, one needs to synthesize data from Wuthnow 1996, 2002; Ladd 1999; Skocpol 2003; and Small 2009.

42 See Allen 2012a.

43 Let me provide an example of the relationship between the science and art of associations. Colleagues from the MacArthur Foundation Youth and Participatory Politics Research Network and I have developed design principles to guide the use and construction of digital tools whose purpose is to engage youth in equitable and efficacious civic or political action. These design principles are available at http://ypp.dmlcentral .net/projects/digital-platforms-project. This project synthesized three years of research on youth participatory experience, "the science of associations," in order to generate these principles as guidance for the "art of association."

44 Bromberg 2011.

45 Anderson 2010.

46 Eng and Han 2000, 2006; Bromberg 2011.

47 I take this up in collaboration with sociologist Angel Parham in Allen and Parham 2015.

48 Allen 2015.

49 See Allen 2010, Allen 2014a, and Woodley 2015. See also how Adbusters, which founded Occupy Wall Street, describes its project of "culture jamming": "We are a global network of culture jammers and creatives working to change the way information flows, the way corporations wield power, and the way meaning is produced in our society" (a description taken from the Adbusters website, accessed May 23, 2012, http://www .adbusters.org). "Cultural jamming is defined as artistic 'terrorism' directed against the information society in which we live . . . The term [culture-jamming] was originally coined by a band by the name of Negativland in 1984. They define it as 'media about media about media' which describes 'billboard alteration and other underground art that seeks to shed light on the dark side of the computer age'" (Lievrouw 2011, p. 72).

50 Peter Levine of Tufts University made the case that civic education now requires teach-

ing students to master the "architecture of the Internet" at an August 2014 American Political Science Association panel on civic education.

51 Wolfinger and Rosenstone 1980; Verba and Schlozman 1995; Levinson 2012.

52 On the negative impact of college on the participatory readiness of women, see Kawashima-Ginsberg and Thomas 2013.

53 On socioeconomic effects, see Nie et al. 1996, Campbell 2009, and Sondheimer and Green 2010.

54 Hillygus 2005, pp. 25–47. Additional tantalizing evidence is available in the work of David Kidd and Emanuele Castano on the relationship between reading literary fiction and the "theory of mind" function. See Kidd and Castano 2013.

55 At the end of *Citizenship across the Curriculum* (Smith 2010), David Scobey laments "the one real lacuna in the book's disciplinary range: attention to the role of the arts and humanities in civic life and civic education." (Nowacek 2010, pp. 2852–53).

56 Smith 2010, pp. 1475–84.

57 Acemoglu and Robinson 2015, p. 1.

58 Shorris 2000, 2013; Hirschman 2009.

COMMENT 1

1 Rawls 1955. See also Rawls 1999, pp. 47–50.

2 See Larmore 1990; Rawls 1993.

COMMENT 2

1 Durkheim 2009.

2 Dewey's best-known line qua education is preceded by an overlooked articulation of education's democratic ends: "I believe that the school is primarily a social institution. Education being a social process, the school is simply that form of community life in which all those agencies are concentrated that will be most effective in bringing the child to share in the inherited resources of the race, and to use his own powers for social ends. I believe that education, therefore, is a process of living and not a preparation for future living" (Dewey 1897).

3 Mantovani 2014.

4 Economists also have a place of privilege and ascendancy at education's "barricades"; Greg Duncan and Richard Murnane come to mind.

5 An approximation might be ideas relating to the mysterious source that generates "influence, authority, and efficacy—the power to perform in a given situation."

6 Of course individual philosophers continue to do extraordinarily important work toiling in education fields. However, seldom are they housed in schools of education, which says it all. Danielle Allen gathered many of the leading philosophers of education during the yearlong seminar she convened at the Institute for Advanced Study, Princeton. See Allen and Reich 2013.

7 Heckman 2013.

8 Ibid.

9 See Sachs 2015.

10 See Lipina 2013.

11 Heckman 2013.

12 See Autor 2014.

13 See Porter 2014.

14 See Evans 2015.

15 See Credit Suisse 2014.

16 Piketty 2014, p. 71.

17 See Cohen et al. 2007.

18 Over 175 years ago, a young Charles Darwin, in a furiously creative phase, jotted down a forgotten note in one of his evolution notebooks: "Educate all classes [educate men and women], improve the women ([and] double the influence) and mankind must improve."

19 See LeVine et al. 2012.

20 See Sachs 2015.

21 See Murphey 2014.

22 See Fry and Hugo 2012.

23 See Reese et al. 1995.

24 Rumbaut 1995.

25 See Rieder 1998.

26 In affluent countries worldwide, poverty among children of immigrants has increased steadily in recent years, with gaps between native-born and immigrants ranging from 7 percent in Australia and Germany to 12 percent in the United States and to 26–28 percent in England and France (Hernandez et al. 2009). Differences among ethnic groups are also prevalent.

27 See Therrien and Ramirez 2001.

28 See Fry and Gonzales 2008.

29 See Capps et al. 2001.

30 See Weissbourd 1996; Luthar 2003.

31 See Kneebone 2014.

32 See Orfield and Lee 2005.

33 See Passel 2006.

34 See Suárez-Orozco 2014.

35 See Suárez-Orozco et al. 2011.

36 See Yoshikawa 2012.

37 Yoshikawa 2012; Suárez-Orozco et al. 2011.

38 See Portes 1999.

39 "Happy families are all alike; every unhappy family is unhappy in its own way" (Tolstoy 2000).

40 See Porter 2014.

41 Suárez-Orozco and Suárez-Orozco 1995.

42 Malin et al. 2014.

COMMENT 3

1 US Department of Education 1983.

2 See, for example, Schudson 1998.

3 National Center on Education Statistics 2013.

4 For a discussion of the role of the courts in educational policy making and their specific role in the state court education adequacy cases, see Rebell and Block 1982; Rebell 2009.

5 411 U.S. 1 (1973).

6 N.Y. Const. Art XI, § 1. The specific provision in the New York constitution states that "the legislature shall provide for the maintenance and support of a system of free common schools, wherein all of the children of this state may be educated." The New York Court of Appeals has interpreted the concept of "educated" to mean "a sound basic education." Levittown v. Nyquist, 439 N.E.2d 359, 368–69 (1982).

7 N.J. Const. Art. IV, § 1.

8 Wash. Const. Art. IX, § 1.

9 Fla. Const. Art. IX, § 1.

10 Robinson v. Cahill, 303 A. 2d 273, 295 (N.J. 1973).

11 Edgewood Indep. Sch. Dist v. Kirby, 777 S.W.2d 391, 395–96 (Tex. 1989).

12 Campbell County School District v. State, 907 P.2d 1238, 1259 (WY. 2001).

13 Conn. Coal. for Justice in Educ. Funding, Inc. v. Rell, 990 A.2d 206, 253 (Conn. 2010).

14 Rose v. Council for Better Education, 790 S.W.2d 186, 212 (KY 1989).

15 Campaign for Fiscal Equity, Inc. v. State, 655 N.E.2d 661 (N.Y. 1995) (CFE II); Campaign for Fiscal Equity v. State, 801 N.E.2d 326 (N.Y. 2003) (CFE II); and Campaign for Fiscal Equity, Inc. v. State, 861 N.E.2d 50 (N.Y. 2006) ("*CFE III*").

16 719 N.Y.S.2d at 485.

COMMENT 4

1 Shklovsky 1925.

2 Ibid.

3 Cruz 2003.

4 Rich 1984.

5 Kroetz 1993.

RESPONSE TO COMMENTATORS

1 Mill 2006 [1859]: 15–16: "The principle requires liberty of tastes and pursuits; of framing the plan of life to suit our own character; of doing as we like, subject to such consequences as may follow . . . Each is the proper guardian of his own health, whether bodily, or mental and spiritual."

2 Mill 2006 [1859]: 76: "With respect to his own feelings and circumstances, the most ordinary man or woman has means of knowledge immeasurably surpassing those that can be possessed by any one else."

3 Bourdieu 1977.

4 "Borges and I" in Bidart 1997.

5 This account of how our mental faculties intersect with our human development derives from the coding structure derived from the Humanities and Liberal Arts Assessment Research (HULA) project, for which I am the principal investigator. The coding
structure is detailed in our "Report on Thirty Years of Grant-Making by the Illinois
Humanities Council," which is available by request to the author.

6 Berlin 1990 [1958]; Mill 2006 [1859].

7 Arendt 1958; Sen 1999.

8 Reich, in progress.

9 Brighouse and Swift 2013.

10 Empirical work tells against the common "creaming" worry: Zimmer et al. 2011. See
also Zimmer and Guarino 2013.

REFERENCES

Acemoglu, Daron, and James A. Robinson. 2015. "The Rise and Decline of General Laws of Capitalism." *Journal of Economic Perspectives* 29(1): 3–28.

Alinksy, Saul. 1971. *Rules for Radicals*. New York: Random House.

Allen, Danielle. 2004a. "A Multilingual America?" *Soundings* 87: 259–80.

———. 2004b. *Talking to Strangers: Anxieties of Citizenship since* Brown v. Board of Education. Chicago: University of Chicago Press.

———. 2010a. "What 'Tuition' and 'Fees' Leaves Out on College Costs." *Washington Post*, December 19. http://www.washingtonpost.com/wp-dyn/content/article/2010/12/17/AR2010121705587.html.

———. 2010b. *Why Plato Wrote*. New Jersey: Wiley-Blackwell.

———. 2011. "Education and Equality." Lecture given at the Institute for Advanced Study, November 16, Princeton, NJ. https://www.youtube.com/watch?v=zrW6HNi9-QU.

———. 2012a. "Art of Association: The Formation of Egalitarian Social Capital." Annual equality lecture for British Sociological Association, April 15, 2012, British Library Conference Centre, London. https://www.youtube.com/watch?v=hZJA6uOS-jk.

———. 2012b. "Helping Students Find Their Place in the World." *Washington Post*, September 23. http://www.washingtonpost.com/opinions/helping-students-find-their-place-in-the-world/2012/09/23/64552334-029a-11e2-8102-ebee9c66e190_story.html.

———. 2013a. "Democracy and Education: Three Principles?" Unpublished essay.

———. 2013b. "Talent Is Everywhere." In *The Future of Affirmative Action: New Paths to Higher Education Diversity after* Fisher v. University of Texas, edited by D. Kahlenberg, 145–59.

———. 2013c. "What We Should Be Doing with Diversity on Our College Campuses?" *Institute Letter*, Summer. http://www.ias.edu/files/pdfs/publications/letter-2013-summer.pdf.

———. 2014a. "Discourse Ethics for Divided Publics." Unpublished essay.

———. 2014b. *Our Declaration: A Reading of the Declaration of Independence in Defense of Equality*. New York: Norton/Liveright.

———. 2015. "Re-conceptualizing Public Spheres." In *From Voice to Influence*, edited by Danielle Allen and Jennifer Light, 178–210. Chicago: University of Chicago.

Allen, Danielle, and Jennifer Light, eds. 2015. *From Voice to Influence*. Chicago: University of Chicago Press.

Allen, Danielle, and Angel Parham. 2015. "Achieving Rooted Cosmopolitanism in a Digital Age." In *From Voice to Influence*, edited by Danielle Allen and Jennifer Light, 254–72. Chicago: University of Chicago Press.

Allen, Danielle, and Robert Reich, eds. 2013. *Education, Justice, and Democracy.* Chicago: University of Chicago Press.

Allensworth, Elaine, and John Q. Easton. 2005. *The On-Track Indicator as a Predictor of High School Graduation.* Chicago: University of Chicago Consortium on Chicago School Research. http://ccsr.uchicago.edu/publications/p78.pdf.

———. 2007. *What Matters for Staying On-Track and Graduating in Chicago Public Schools.* Chicago: University of Chicago Consortium on Chicago School Research. http://ccsr.uchicago.edu/sites/default/files/publications/07%20What%20Matters %20Final.pdf.

Allensworth, Elaine, Julia A. Gwynne, Paul Moore, and Marisa de la Torre. 2014. *Looking Forward to High School and College: Middle Grade Indicators of Readiness in Chicago Public Schools.* Chicago: University of Chicago Consortium on Chicago School Research.

American Academy of Arts and Sciences. 2009. *Introducing the Humanities Indicators: An Online Prototype of National Data Collection in the Humanities.* Cambridge, MA: American Academy of Arts and Sciences.

———. 2013. *The Heart of the Matter.* Cambridge, MA: American Academy of Arts and Sciences.

American Council of Learned Societies. 1985. *A Report to the Congress of the United States on the State of the Humanities and the Reauthorization of the National Endowment for the Humanities.* New York: American Council of Learned Societies.

Anderson, Elizabeth. 2007. "Fair Opportunity in Education: A Democratic Equality Perspective." *Ethics* 117(4): 595–622.

———. 2010. *The Imperative of Integration.* Princeton, NJ: Princeton University Press.

Arendt, H. 1958. *The Human Condition.* Chicago: University of Chicago Press.

———. 1959. "Reflections on Little Rock." *Dissent* 6(1): 45–56.

———. 1968. *Men in Dark Times.* New York: Harcourt Brace.

Arum, Richard, and Josipa Roska. 2011. *Academically Adrift.* Chicago: University of Chicago Press.

Association of American Colleges and Universities. 2015. "AACU Civic Engagement Rubrics." http://www.aacu.org/value-rubrics.

Autor, D. 2014. "Skills, Education, and the Rise of Earnings Inequality among the 'Other 99 Percent.'" *Science* 344(6186): 843–51.

Bachen, Christine, Chad Raphael, Kathleen-M. Lynn, Kristen McKee, and Jessica Philippi. 2008. "Civic Engagement, Pedagogy, and Information Technology on Web Sites for Youth." *Political Communication* 25(3): 290–310.

Banaji, Shakuntala. 2011. "Framing Young Citizens: Explicit Invitation and Implicit Exclusion on Youth Civic Websites." *Language and Intercultural Communication* 11(2): 126–41.

Bennett, Lance, Chris Wells, and Deen Freelon. 2009. "Communicating Citizenship Online: Models of Civic Learning in the Youth Web Sphere." Civic Learning Online Project. http://www.engagedyouth.org.

Bennett, Lance, and Michael Xenos. 2005. "Young Voters and the Web of Politics 2004: The Youth Political Web Sphere Comes of Age." CIRCLE Working Paper 42. http:// www.civicyouth.org/PopUps/WorkingPapers/WP42BennettXenos.pdf.

Berlin, Isaiah. 1990 [1958]. *Four Essays on Liberty*. Oxford: Oxford University Press.

Berman, S. 1997. "Civil Society and the Collapse of the Weimar Republic." *World Politics* 49(3): 401–29.

Bidart, Frank. 1997. *Desire*. New York: Farrar, Straus & Giroux.

Billington, Josie. 2011. "'Reading for Life': Prison Reading Groups in Practice and Theory." *Critical Survey* 23: 67–85.

Blank, Rolf. K. 2010. *State Growth Models for School Accountability*. Washington, DC: Council of Chief State School Officers.

Bourdieu, Pierre. 1977. *Outline of a Theory of Practice*, translated by Richard Nice. Cambridge: Cambridge University Press.

Bowles, S., G. Loury, and R. Sethi. 2009. "Group Inequality." Working paper. Retrieved October 4, 2010, from http://www.columbia.edu/~rs328/GroupInequality.pdf.

Boyer, John, ed. 1997. *The Aims of Education: The College of the University of Chicago*. Chicago: University of Chicago Press.

Brighouse, Harry, and A. Swift. 2013. "Family Values and School Policy: Shaping Values and Conferring Advantage." In *Education, Justice, and Democracy*, edited by Danielle Allen and Robert Reich, 199–220. Chicago: University of Chicago Press.

Brodhead, Richard. 2011. "In Praise of the Humanities and the 'Fire That Never Goes Out.'" *Duke Today*, October 23.

———. 2012. "Advocating for the Humanities." *Duke Today*, March 19.

Bromberg, Philip. 2011. *The Shadow of the Tsunami and the Growth of the Relational Mind*. New York: Routledge.

Broughton, Janet. 2010. "Commencement for Programs in Celtic, Comparative Literature, Dutch, French, German, Italian, Portuguese, Scandinavian, Slavic, Spanish." Commencement address delivered at University of California, Berkeley.

Campaign for Fiscal Equity v. State of New York I. 1995. 86 N.Y.2d 307.

Campbell, D. E. 2009. "Civic Engagement and Education: An Empirical Test of the Sorting Model." *American Journal of Political Science* 53(4): 771–86.

Capps, Randolph, Michael E. Fix, and Jane Reardon-Anderson. 2003. "Children of Immigrants Show Slight Reductions in Poverty, Hardship." http://www.urban.org /sites/default/files/alfresco/publication-pdfs/310887-Children-of-Immigrants-Show -Slight-Reductions-in-Poverty-Hardship.pdf.

Cavell, S. 1999. *The Claim of Reason: Wittgenstein, Skepticism, Morality, and Tragedy*. Oxford: Oxford University Press.

Childress, Stacey, Monica Higgins, Ann Ishimaru, and Sola Takahashi. 2011. "Managing for Results at the New York City Department of Education." In *Education Reform in New York City: Ambitious Change in the Nation's Most Complex School System*, edited by Jennifer A. O'Day, Catherine S. Bitter, and Louis M. Gomez, 87–108. Cambridge, MA: Harvard Education.

CIRCLE Staff. 2013. "The Youth Vote in 2012." CIRCLE Fact Sheet. http://www.civic youth.org/wp-content/uploads/2013/05/CIRCLE_2013FS_outhVoting2012FINAL .pdf.

Cohen, G. E. 2009. *Rescuing Justice and Equality*. Cambridge, MA: Harvard University Press.

Cohen, Joel E., David E. Bloom, and Martin B. Malin, eds. 2007. *Educating All Children: A Global Agenda*. Cambridge, MA: MIT Press.

Commission on the Humanities. 1980. *The Humanities in American Life: Report of the Commission on the Humanities*. Berkeley: University of California Press. http://ark .cdlib.org/ark:/13030/ft8j49p1jc/.

Committee on Prospering in the Global Economy of the Twenty-First Century, National Academy of Sciences, National Academy of Engineering, Institute of Medicine. 2007. *Rising above the Gathering Storm: Energizing and Employing America for a Brighter Economic Future*. Washington, DC: The National Academies Press.

Credit Suisse. 2014. *Global Wealth Data Book*, accessed August 15, 2010. https:// publications.credit-suisse.com/tasks/render/file/?fileID=5521F296-D460-2B88 -081889DB12817E02.

Cruz, Nilo. 2003. *Anna in the Tropics*. New York: Theatre Communications Group.

Darling-Hammond, Linda, and R. Weingarten. 2014. "It's Time for a New Accountability in American Education." *The Huffington Post*, May 19.

Dawood, Y. 2008. "The Anti-domination Model and the Judicial Oversight of Democracy." *Georgetown Law Journal* 96: 1411–85.

Dee, T. 2003. "Are There Civic Returns to Education?" CIRCLE Working Paper 8. College Park, MD: The Center for Information and Research on Civic Learning and Engagement.

Delbanco, Andrew. 2012. *College: What It Was, Is, and Should Be*. Princeton, NJ: Princeton University Press.

de Tocqueville, A. 1990 [1835–1840]. *Democracy in America*. New York: Vintage Classics.

Dewey, John. 1897. "My Pedagogic Creed." *The School Journal* 54(3).

Douglas, W. O. 1963. "The Right of Association." *Columbia Law Review* 63(8): 1361–83.

Doumas, Leonidas, and John Hummel. 2005. "Approaches to Modeling Human Mental Representations: What Works, What Doesn't, and Why." In *The Cambridge Handbook of Thinking and Reasoning*, edited by Keith Holyoak and Robert Morrison, 73–94. New York: Cambridge University Press.

DuBois, W. E. B. 1903. *The Souls of Black Folk*. New York: Library of America.

Durkheim, Émile. 2009. *Sociology and Philosophy*. London: Taylor & Francis.

Emerson, T. I. 1964. "Freedom of Association and Freedom of Expression." *Yale Law Journal* 74: 1–35.

Eng, David, and Shinhee Han. 2000. "A Dialogue on Racial Melancholia." *Psychoanalytic Dialogues: The International Journal of Relational Perspectives* 10(4): 667–700.

————. 2006. "Desegregating Love: Transnational Adoption, Racial Reparation, and Racial Transitional Objects." *Studies in Gender and Sexuality* 7(2): 141–72.

Evans, Christine. 2015. "Save the Wisconsin Idea." *The New York Times*, February 16. http://www.nytimes.com/2015/02/16/opinion/save-the-wisconsin-idea.html?hp& action=click&pgtype=Homepage&module=c-column-top-span-region&region=c -column-top-span-region&WT.nav=c-column-top-span-region&_r=0.

Fry, Richard, and Felisa Gonzales. 2008. "A Profile of Hispanic Public School Students." http://www.pewhispanic.org/2008/08/26/one-in-five-and-growing-fast-a-profile-of -hispanic-public-school-students/.

Fry, Richard, and Mark Hugo Lopez. 2012. "Hispanic Student Enrollments Reach New Highs in 2011." http://www.pewhispanic.org/2012/08/20/hispanic-student -enrollments-reach-new-highs-in-2011.

Galison, P. 1997. *Image and Logic: A Material Culture of Microphysics*. Chicago: University of Chicago Press.

Gardner, Howard. 1983. *Good Work: When Excellence and Ethics Meet*. New York: Basic Books.

————. 2011. *Frames of Mind: The Theory of Multiple Intelligences*. New York: Basic Books.

————. 2015. "In Defense of Disinterestedness." In *From Voice to Influence*, edited by Danielle Allen and Jennifer Light, 232–53. Chicago: University of Chicago Press.

Gerodimos, Roman. 2008. "Mobilising Young Citizens in the UK: A Content Analysis of Youth and Issue Websites." *Information, Communication, and Society* 11(7): 964–88.

————. 2010. "New Media, New Citizens: The Terms and Conditions of Online Youth Civic Engagement." PhD dissertation, Bournemouth University.

Glaeser, Edward L., Giacomo Ponzetto, and Andrei Shleifer. 2006. "Why Does Democracy Need Education?" NBER Working Paper No. 12128.

Goldin, Claudia, and L. Katz. 2008. *The Race between Education and Technology*. Cambridge, MA: Belknap Press.

Goldstone, Robert, and Ji Son. 2005. "Similarity." In *The Cambridge Handbook of Thinking and Reasoning*, edited by Keith Holyoak and Robert Morrison, 13–36. New York: Cambridge University Press.

Gutmann, A., ed. 1998. *Freedom of Association*. Princeton, NJ: Princeton University Press.

————. 1999. *Democratic Education*. Princeton, NJ: Princeton University Press.

————. 2015. "What Makes a University Education Worthwhile?" In *The Aims of Higher Education: Problems of Morality and Justice*, edited by M. McPherson and H. Brighouse, 7–25. Chicago: University of Chicago Press.

Hayward, Clarissa. 2013. *How Americans Make Race: Stories, Institutions, Spaces*. New York: Cambridge University Press.

Heckman, James. 2013. "The President's Early Childhood Plan Makes Great Sense." *The New York Times*, February 25. http://www.nytimes.com/roomfordebate/2013/02

/25/is-public-preschool-a-smart-investment/the-presidents-early-childhood-plan
-makes-great-sense.

Heiland, Donna, and Laura Rosenthal. 2011. *Literary Study, Measurement, and the Sublime: Disciplinary Assessment.* New York: Teagle Foundation.

Hernandez, Donald J., Nancy A. Denton, and Suzanne Macartney. 2009. *Children in Immigrant Families: The U.S. and 50 States: Economic Need beyond the Official Poverty Measure.* Albany, NY: Center for Social and Demographic Analysis.

Hess, Diana. 2009. *Controversy in the Classroom: The Democratic Power of Discussion.* New York: Routledge.

Hess, Diana, and P. McAvoy. 2012. *The Political Classroom: Ethics and Evidence in Democratic Education.* New York: Routledge.

Hillygus, D. Sunshine. 2005. "The Missing Link: Exploring the Relationship between Higher Education and Political Engagement." *Political Behavior* 27(1): 25–47.

Hirschman, Sarah. 2009. *People and Stories: Who Owns Literature? Communities Find Their Voice through Short Stories.* Bloomington, IN: iUniverse.

Holyoak, Keith, and Robert Morrison, eds. 2005. *The Cambridge Handbook of Thinking and Reasoning.* New York: Cambridge University Press.

Honneth, Axel. 1992. "Integrity and Disrespect: Principles of a Conception of Morality Based on a Theory of Recognition." *Political Theory* 20(2): 187–201.

Inclan, Jaime. 1997. "Evaluation of Clemente Course." In *New American Blues*, edited by Earl Shorris, 402–9. New York: W. W. Norton.

Jackson, Philip. 1968. *Life in Classrooms.* New York: Holt, Rinehart & Winston.

Jay, Paul, and Gerald Graff. 2012. "Fear of Being Useful." *Inside Higher Education*, January 5. http://www.insidehighered.com/views/2012/01/05/essay-new-approach
-defend-value-humanities#.T0Tw_WhErgk.facebook.

Kahlenberg, D., ed. 2013. *The Future of Affirmative Action: New Paths to Higher Education Diversity after* Fisher v. University of Texas. Washington, DC: Century Foundation.

Karp, Stan. 2012. "Taking Teacher Quality Seriously: A Collaborative Approach to Teacher Evaluation." *Rethinking Schools*, Summer, 46–50.

Katz, Michael. 1976. *A History of Compulsory Education Laws.* Fastback series, no. 75, bicentennial series. Bloomington, IN: Phi Delta Kappa.

Kaufman, James, and Robert Sternberg, eds. 2010. *The Cambridge Handbook of Creativity.* Cambridge: Cambridge University Press.

Kawashima-Ginsberg, K., and N. Thomas. 2013. "Civic Engagement and Political Leadership among Women—a Call for Solutions." CIRCLE Fact Sheet. http://www
.civicyouth.org/wp-content/uploads/2013/05/Gender-and-Political-Leadership-Fact
-Sheet-3.pdf.

Keohane, Nannerl. 2012. "The Liberal Arts as Signposts in the 21st Century." *Chronicle of Higher Education*, January 29. http://chronicle.com/article/The-Liberal-Arts-as
-Guideposts/130475/.

Kidd, David, and Emanuele Castano. 2013. "Reading Literary Fiction Improves Theory of Mind." *Science* 342 (6156): 377–80.

Kiley, Kevin. 2012. "Making the Case." *Inside Higher Education*, November 19. http:// www.insidehighered.com/news/2012/11/19/liberal-arts-colleges-rethink-their -messaging-face-criticism.

Kneebone, Elizabeth. 2014. "The Growth and Spread of Concentrated Poverty, 2000 to 2008–2012." http://www.brookings.edu/research/interactives/2014/concentrated -poverty#/M10420.

Kohlberg, Lawrence. 1970. "The Moral Atmosphere of the School." In *The Unstudied Curriculum: Its Impact on Children*, edited by Norman Overly, 104–239. Washington, DC: Association for Supervision and Curriculum Development.

Koppelman, A. 2004. "Should Noncommercial Associations Have an Absolute Right to Discriminate?" *Law and Contemporary Problems* 67(4): 27–57.

Kroetz, Frank Xaver. 1993. *Through the Leaves and Other Plays*, translated by Roger Downey. New York: Theatre Communications Group.

Ladd, Everett. 1999. *The Ladd Report*. Florence, MA: Free Press.

Ladd, H., and S. Loeb. 2013. "The Challenges of Measuring School Quality: Implications for Educational Equity." In *Education, Justice, and Democracy*, edited by Danielle Allen and Robert Reich, 19–42. Chicago: University of Chicago Press.

Laden, Anthony. 2013. "Learning to Be Equal." In *Education, Justice, and Democracy*, edited by Danielle Allen and Robert Reich, 62–79. Chicago: University of Chicago Press.

Lane, Melissa. 1998. *Method and Politics in Plato's Statesman*. Cambridge: Cambridge University Press.

Lareau, Annette. 2011. *Unequal Childhoods: Class, Race, and Family Life*. 2nd edition. Berkeley: University of California Press.

Larmore, Charles. 1990. "Political Liberalism." *Political Theory* 18(3): 339–60.

Lear, Jonathan. 1992. "Inside and Outside the *Republic*." *Phronesis* 37(2): 184–215.

LeBoeuf, Robyn, and Eldar Shafir. 2005. "Decision Making." In *The Cambridge Handbook of Thinking and Reasoning*, edited by Keith Holyoak and Robert Morrison, 243–66. New York: Cambridge University Press.

Levine, Peter, Cynthia Gibson, et al. 2003. *Special Report: The Civic Mission of Schools*. New York: CIRCLE and the Carnegie Corporation of New York.

LeVine, Robert A., et al. 2012. *Literacy and Mothering: How Women's Schooling Changes the Lives of the World's Children*. Oxford: Oxford University Press.

Levinson, Meira. 2012. *No Citizen Left Behind*. Cambridge, MA: Harvard University Press.

Leyton-Brown, K., and Y. Shoham. 2008. *Essentials of Game Theory: A Concise, Multidisciplinary Introduction*. San Rafael, CA: Morgan & Claypool.

Lievrouw, Leah. 2011. *Alternative and Activist New Media*. Cambridge, UK: Polity.

Linder, D. O. 1984. "Freedom of Association after *Roberts v. United States Jaycees*." *Michigan Law Review* 82(8): 1878–1903.

Linkon, Sherry. 2011. *Literary Learning: Teaching in the English Major*. Bloomington: Indiana University Press.

Lipina, Sebastián J. 2013. "Biological and Sociocultural Determinants of Neurocognitive Development: Central Aspects of the Current Scientific Agenda." http://www .casinapioiv.va/content/dam/accademia/pdf/sv125/sv125-lipina.pdf.

Livingstone, Sonia. 2007. "The Challenge of Engaging Youth Online: Contrasting Producers' and Teenagers' Interpretations of Websites." *European Journal of Communication* 22(2): 165–84.

London, J. 2011. "Circle of Justice." *History of Political Thought* 32(3): 425–47.

Lundberg, C. A., and L. A. Schreiner. 2004. "Quality and Frequency of Faculty-Student Interaction as Predictors of Learning: An Analysis by Student Race/Ethnicity." *Journal of College Student Development* 45: 549–65.

Luthar, S. 2003. *Resilience and Vulnerability: Adaptation in the Context of Childhood Adversities*. Cambridge: Cambridge University Press.

Macedo, Stephen, et al. 2005. *Democracy at Risk: How Political Choices Undermine Citizen Participation and What We Can Do about It*. Washington, DC: Brookings Institution.

Malin, Heather, Parissa J. Ballard, Maryam Lucia Attai, Anne Colby, and William Damon. 2014. "Youth Civic Development and Education: A Consensus Report." https://coa.stanford.edu/sites/default/files/Civic%20Education%20report.pdf.

Mantena, K. 2012. "Another Realism: The Politics of Gandhian Nonviolence." *American Political Science Review* 106(455–70).

Mantovani, Sussana. 2014. Keynote address. Presented at the Reggio Children Conference on Early Childhood Education and Globalization. Reggio Children, Reggio Emilia, Italy.

Markell, Patchen. Forthcoming. *Politics Against Rule: Hannah Arendt and* The Human Condition.

Marx, Michael. 2005. "Disciplining the Minds of Students: The Study of English." *Change: The Magazine of Higher Learning*, March/April, 40–42.

Mathae, Katherine, and Catherine Birzer, eds. 2004. *Reinvigorating the Humanities: Enhancing Research and Education on Campus and Beyond*. Washington, DC: Association of American Universities.

McAfee, Noëlle. 2015. "Acting Politically in a Digital Age." In *From Voice to Influence*, edited by Danielle Allen and Jennifer Light, 273–92. Chicago: University of Chicago Press.

McFarland, Daniel, and Reuben Thomas. 2010. "Bowling Young: How Youth Voluntary Associations Influence Adult Political Participation." *American Sociological Review* 71: 401–25.

McGuinn, Patrick. 2010. "No Child Left Behind and the Transformation of Federal Education Policy, 1965–2005." Lecture, Institute for Advanced Study, on file with author.

McPherson, M., and H. Brighouse, eds. 2015. *The Aims of Higher Education: Problems of Morality and Justice*. Chicago: University of Chicago Press.

Menand, Louis. 2010. *The Marketplace of Ideas: Reform and Resistance in the American University*. New York: Norton.

Mill, John S. 2006 [1859]. *On Liberty and Other Writings*. Cambridge: Cambridge University Press.

Milner, Henry. 2010. *The Internet Generation: Engaged Citizens or Political Dropouts*. Medford, MA: Tufts University Press.

Moglen, Seth. 2013. "Sharing Knowledge, Practicing Democracy: A Vision for the Twenty-First-Century University." In *Education, Justice, and Democracy*, edited by Danielle Allen and Robert Reich, 267–84. Chicago: University of Chicago Press.

Morrill, Richard. 2012. "What Is the Value of Liberal Education?" *The Huffington Post*, November 6. http://www.huffingtonpost.com/richard-morrill/liberal-education_b _2083994.html.

Murphey, David. 2014. "America's Hispanic Children: Gaining Ground, Looking Forward." http://www.childtrends.org/wp-content/uploads/2014/09/2014 -38AmericaHispanicChildren.pdf.

Nagda, B. A., S. R. Gregerman, J. Jonides, W. von Hippel, and J. S. Lerner. 1998. "Undergraduate Student-Faculty Research Partnerships Affect Student Retention." *Review of Higher Education* 22: 55–72.

National Center on Education Statistics. 2013. "What Level of Knowledge and Skills Have the Nation's Students Achieved?" http://www.nationsreportcard.gov/reading _math_2013/#/what-knowledge.

National Governors' Association. 2010. "Common Core State Standards Initiative Standards: Setting Criteria." http://www.corestandards.org/assets/Criteria.pdf.

Nie, N. J., J. Junn, and K. Stehlik-Barry. 1996. *Education and Democratic Citizenship in America*. Chicago: University of Chicago Press.

Nowacek, Rebecca S. 2010. "Understanding Citizenship as Vocation in a Multidisciplinary Senior Capstone." In *Citizenship across the Curriculum*, edited by Michael Smith, Rebecca S. Nowacek, and Jeffrey L. Bernstein, 1384–1652. Bloomington: Indiana University Press.

Nussbaum, Martha. 1996. *Poetic Justice: The Literary Imagination and Public Life*. Boston: Beacon Press.

———. 2012. *Not for Profit: Why Democracy Needs the Humanities*. Princeton, NJ: Princeton University Press.

Obama, Barack. 2012. "Remarks by the President at the Democratic National Convention," accessed September 19, 2015. https://www.whitehouse.gov/the-press -office/2012/09/07/remarks-president-democratic-national-convention.

———. 2013. "Remarks by the President in the State of the Union Address," accessed September 19, 2015. https://www.whitehouse.gov/the-press-office/2013/02/12 /remarks-president-state-union-address.

Ober, Josiah. 2007. "Natural Capacities and Democracy as a Good-in-Itself." *Philosophical Studies* 132: 59–73.

———. 2008. *Democracy and Knowledge: Innovation and Learning in Classical Athens.* Princeton, NJ: Princeton University Press.

———. 2010. "What Is Democracy? What Is It Good For?" Presented at James Moffett Lecture, Princeton University, Princeton, NJ, September 30.

Orfield, Gary, and Chungmei Lee. 2005. "Why Segregation Matters: Poverty and Educational Inequality." http://civilrightsproject.ucla.edu/research/k-12-education/integration-and-diversity/why-segregation-matters-poverty-and-educational-inequality.

Passel, Jeffrey. 2006. "Size and Characteristics of the Unauthorized Migrant Population in the U.S." http://pewhispanic.org/reports/report.php?ReportID=61.

Pettit, Philip. 1997. *Republicanism: A Theory of Freedom and Government.* Oxford: Oxford University Press.

Piketty, Thomas. 2014. *Capital in the Twenty-First Century.* Cambridge, MA: Harvard University Press.

Pitkin, H. 2000. *Attack of the Blob: Hannah Arendt's Conception of the Social.* Chicago: University of Chicago Press.

Porter, Eduardo. 2014. "A Simple Equation: More Education = More Income." *The New York Times,* September 10. http://www.nytimes.com/2014/09/11/business/economy/a-simple-equation-more-education-more-income.html?_r=0.

Portes, Alejandro. 1999. "Towards a New World: The Origins and Effects of Transnational Activities." *Ethnic and Racial Studies* 22(2): 463–77.

Prentice, Deborah. 2012. "The Psychology of Social Norms and the Promotion of Human Rights." In *Understanding Social Action, Promoting Human Rights,* edited by Ryan Goodman, Derek Jinks, and Andrew K. Woods. Oxford: Oxford University Press.

Putnam, Robert. 1995. "Bowling Alone: America's Declining Social Capital." *Journal of Democracy* 6(1): 65–78.

———. 2000. *Bowling Alone.* New York: Simon and Schuster.

———. 2007. "*E Pluribus Unum*: Diversity and Community in the Twenty-First Century." *Scandinavian Political Studies* 30(2): 137–74.

Rawlings, Hunter. 2015. "College Is Not a Commodity. Stop Treating It like One." *Washington Post,* June 9.

Rawls, John. 1955. "Two Concepts of Rules." *The Philosophical Review* 64(1): 3–32.

———. 1993. *Political Liberalism.* New York: Columbia University Press.

———. 1999. *A Theory of Justice,* revised edition. Cambridge, MA: Belknap Press.

Rebell, Michael A. 2009. *Courts and Kids: Pursuing Educational Equity through the State Courts.* Chicago: University of Chicago Press.

Rebell, Michael A., and Arthur L. Block. 1982. *Educational Policy Making and the Courts.* Chicago: University of Chicago Press.

Reese, L., S. Balzano, R. Gallimore, and C. Goldenberg. 1995. "The Concept of
    Educación: Latino Family Values and American Schooling." *International Journal of
    Educational Research* 23(1): 57–81.
Reich, Rob. 2013. "Equality, Adequacy, and K–12 Education." In *Education, Justice,
    and Democracy*, edited by Danielle Allen and Robert Reich. Chicago: University of
    Chicago Press.
———. forthcoming. *Just Giving: Toward a Political Theory of Philanthropy.*
Rich, Frank. 1984. "Stage: Through the Leaves." *New York Times*, April 6.
Rieder, Jonathan. 1998. "Border Crossers: A Journalist's Travels through the Latino
    United States." http://www.nytimes.com/books/98/04/12/reviews/980412.12riedert
    .html.
Rips, Lance, and Douglas Medin. 2005. "Concepts and Categories: Memory, Meaning,
    and Metaphysics." In *The Cambridge Handbook of Thinking and Reasoning*, edited by
    Keith Holyoak and Robert Morrison, 37–72. New York: Cambridge University Press.
Robins, Philip, and Murat Aydede, eds. 2009. *The Cambridge Handbook of Situated
    Cognition.* New York: Cambridge University Press.
Romney, Mitt. 2012. "Full Text of Speech to GOP Convention," accessed September 19,
    2015. http://www.washingtonpost.com/politics/rnc-2012-mitt-romney-speech-to
    -gop-convention-excerpts/2012/08/30/7d575ee6-f2ec-11e1-a612-3cfc842a6d89_story
    .html.
Rose, Mike. 2012. "Heal the Academic-Vocational Schism." *Chronicle of Higher
    Education*, September 10.
Rothstein, R. 2013. "Racial Segregation and Black Student Achievement." In *Education,
    Justice, and Democracy*, edited by Danielle Allen and Robert Reich, 173–98. Chicago:
    University of Chicago Press.
Rumbaut, R. 1995. "The New Californians: Comparative Research Findings on the
    Educational Progress of Immigrant Children." In *California's Immigrant Children*,
    edited by R. Rumbaut and W. Cornelius. La Jolla, CA: Center for US-Mexican
    Studies.
Sachs, Jeffrey. 2015. "Financing Education for All." Project Syndicate. http://www
    .project-syndicate.org/commentary/financing-education-poor-children-by-jeffrey
    -d-sachs-2015-03.
Salovey, Peter, and David Sluyter, eds. 1997. *Emotional Development and Emotional
    Intelligence: Implications for Educators.* New York: Basic Books.
Sanders, S., ed. 2006. *Margins of Writing, Origins of Cultures: Unofficial Writing in the
    Ancient Near East and Beyond.* Chicago: University of Chicago Press.
Schudson, Michael. 1998. *The Good Citizen: A History of American Civic Life.* Florence,
    MA: Free Press.
———. 2003. "Click Here for Democracy: A History and Critique of an Information-
    Based Model of Citizenship." In *Democracy and New Media*, edited by H. Jenkins,
    49–59. Cambridge, MA: MIT Press.

Sen, Amartya. 1999. *Development as Freedom*. New York: Knopf.

Sennett, Richard. 2008. *The Craftsman*. New Haven, CT: Yale University Press.

Shklovsky, Viktor. 1925. "Art as Technique." http://paradise.caltech.edu/ist4/lectures /Viktor_Sklovski_Art_as_Technique.pdf.

Shorris, Earl. 2000. *Riches for the Poor: The Clemente Course in the Humanities*. New York: W. W. Norton.

———. 2013. *The Art of Freedom: Teaching Humanities to the Poor*. New York: W. W. Norton.

Shulman, G. 2008. *American Prophecy: Race and Redemption in American Culture*. Minneapolis: University of Minnesota Press.

Skocpol, T. 2003. *Diminished Democracy: From Membership to Management in American Civic Life*. Rothbaum series. Norman: University of Oklahoma Press.

Small, Mario. 2009. *Unanticipated Gains: Origins of Network Inequality in Everyday Life*. Oxford: Oxford University Press.

Smith, Michael, Rebecca S. Nowacek, and Jeffrey L. Bernstein. 2010. *Citizenship across the Curriculum*. Bloomington: Indiana University Press.

Soifer, A. 1998. *Law and the Company We Keep*. Cambridge, MA: Harvard University Press.

Sondheimer, R. M., and D. P. Green. 2010. "Using Experiments to Estimate the Effects of Education on Voter Turnout." *American Journal of Political Science* 54(1): 174–89.

Sternberg, Robert, and Scott Kaufman, eds. 2011. *The Cambridge Handbook of Intelligence*. New York: Cambridge University Press.

Sternberg, Robert, Todd Lubart, James Kaufman, and Jean Pretz. 2005. "Creativity." In *The Cambridge Handbook of Thinking and Reasoning*, edited by Keith Holyoak and Robert Morrison, 315–70. New York: Cambridge University Press.

Stout, J. 2004. *Democracy and Tradition*. Princeton, NJ: Princeton University Press.

Suárez-Orozco, Carola, and Marcelo Suárez-Orozco. 1995. *Transformations: Immigration, Family Life, and Achievement Motivation among Latino Adolescents*. Stanford, CA: Stanford University Press.

———. 2013. "Conferring Disadvantage: Immigration, Schools, and the Family." In *Education, Justice, and Democracy*, edited by Danielle Allen and Robert Reich, 133–54. Chicago: University of Chicago Press.

Suárez-Orozco, Carola, Hirokazu Yoshikawa, Robert T. Teranishi, and Marcelo M. Suárez-Orozco. 2011. "Growing Up in the Shadows: The Developmental Implications of Unauthorized Status." http://hepg.org/her-home/issues/harvard-educational -review-volume-81-number-3/herarticle/the-developmental-implications-of -unauthorized-sta.

Suárez-Orozco, M. 2014. "Las Tres Caras de Herodes: Éxodo de Criaturas, Migraciones Catastróficas y Vida en Sombras." http://www.pass.va/content/dam/scienzesociali /pdf/ninosmigrantes.pdf.

Sundquist, Eric. 2012. "The Humanities and the National Interest," *American Literary History* 24(3): 590–607.

Szreter, S., and M. Woolcock. 2004. "Health by Association? Social Capital, Social Theory, and the Political Economy of Public Health." *International Journal of Epidemiology* 33(4): 650–67.

Tarrow, S. 1996. "Making Social Science Work across Space and Time: A Critical Reflection on Robert Putnam's *Making Democracy Work*." *American Political Science Review* 90: 389–97.

Therrien, Melissa, and R. Ramirez. 2001. *The Hispanic Population in the United States: Population Characteristics, March 2000*. Current Population Reports, US Census Bureau. Washington, DC: Government Printing Office.

Tinto, V. 1993. *Leaving College: Rethinking the Causes and Curses of Student Attrition*. 2nd edition. Chicago: University of Chicago Press.

Tolstoy, Leo. 2000. *Anna Karenina*, translated by Richard Pevear and Larissa Volokhonsky. New York: Penguin Classics.

Tversky, Barbara. 2005. "Visuospatial Reasoning." In *The Cambridge Handbook of Thinking and Reasoning*, edited by Keith Holyoak and Robert Morrison, 209–42. New York: Cambridge University Press.

University of Chicago Consortium on Chicago School Research. "Graduation and School Culture: What Matters in the Freshman Year." CCSR Report, accessed August 15, 2010. https://ccsr.uchicago.edu/ssr/school/1777/high/2009/report/report-freshman/section-freshman-intro.html.

US Department of Education. 1983. "A Nation at Risk." Retrieved from http://www2.ed.gov/pubs/NatAtRisk/risk.html.

US Department of Education, National Center for Educational Statistics. 2006. "Baccalaureate and Beyond Longitudinal Study." Report by Jennifer Wine, Melissa Cominole, Sara Wheeless, Kristin Dudley, and Jeff Franklin. NCES 2006–166. Washington, DC: Government Printing Office.

———. 2011. "Baccalaureate and Beyond Longitudinal Study." Report by Emily Cataldi, Caitlin Green, Robin Henke, Terry Lew, Jennie Woo, Bryan Shepherd, and Peter Siegel. NCES 2011–236. Washington, DC: Government Printing Office.

US House of Representatives. 1945. *Proceedings of the 45th National Encampment of the Veterans of Foreign Wars of the United States, August 22–24, 1944* (H. Doc. 182). Text from *Congressional Documents*, available from ProQuest Congressional, accessed January 27, 2012.

———. *Proceedings of the 79th National Convention of the Veterans of Foreign Wars of the United States* (H. Doc. 96-100). Text from *Congressional Documents*, available from ProQuest Congressional, accessed January 27, 2012.

US Supreme Court. 1958. *NAACP v. Alabama ex rel Patterson*. 357 U.S. 449.

———. 1961. *International Association of Machinists et al., Appellants, v. S. B. Street et al.* 367 U.S. 740.

———. 1963. *NAACP v. Button*. 371 U.S. 415.

———. 1973. *Tillman v. Wheaton-Haven Recreation Assn, Inc.* 410 U.S. 431.

———. 1976. *Runyon et Ux., DBA Bobbe's School v. McCrary et al.* 427 U.S. 160.

———. 1984. *Roberts v Jaycees*. 468 U.S. 609.

———. 1987. *Board of Directors, Rotary International v. Rotary Club of Duarte*. 481 U.S. 537.

Van Oorschot, W., W. Arts, and J. Gelissen. 2006. "Social Capital in Europe: Measurement and Social and Regional Distribution of a Multifaceted Phenomenon." *Acta Sociologica* 49(2): 159–67.

Verba, Sidney, and Kay Lehman Schlozman. 1995. *Voice and Equality: Civic Voluntarism in American Politics*. Cambridge, MA: Harvard University Press.

Volkwein, J., and D. Carbone. 1994. "The Impact of Departmental Research and Teaching Climates on Undergraduate Growth and Satisfaction." *Journal of Higher Education* 65: 146–67.

Walton, Gregory. 2013. "The Myth of Intelligence: Smartness Isn't Like Height." In *Education, Justice, and Democracy*, edited by Danielle Allen and Robert Reich, 155–72. Chicago: University of Chicago Press.

Warren, M. E. 2000. *Democracy and Association*. Princeton, NJ: Princeton University Press.

Wei, Ian. 2012. *Intellectual Culture in Medieval Paris*. Cambridge: Cambridge University Press.

Weissbourd, Richard. 1996. *The Vulnerable Child*. Boston: Da Capo Press.

Wineburg, Samuel. 1999. *Historical Thinking and Other Unnatural Acts: Charting the Future of Teaching the Past*. Philadelphia, PA: Temple University Press.

Winerip, Michael. 2011. "Helping Teachers Help Themselves." *New York Times*, June 11.

Wolfinger, Raymond, and Steven Rosenstone. 1980. *Who Votes?* New Haven, CT: Yale University Press.

Woodly, Deva. 2015. *The Politics of Common Sense: How Social Movements Use Public Discourse to Change Politics and Win Acceptance*. Oxford: Oxford University Press.

Woods, Christopher. 2006. "Bilingualism, Scribal Learning, and the Death of Sumerian." In *Margins of Writing, Origins of Cultures: Unofficial Writing in the Ancient near East and Beyond*, edited by S. Sanders, 91–120. Chicago: University of Chicago Press.

Wuthnow, Robert. 1996. *Sharing the Journey: Support Groups and the Quest for a New Community*. Florence, MA: Free Press.

———. 2002. *Loose Connections: Joining Together in America's Fragmented Communities*. Cambridge, MA: Harvard University Press.

Xenos, Michael, and Lance Bennett. 2007. "The Disconnection in Online Politics: The Youth Political Web Sphere and US Election Sites, 2002–2004." *Information, Communication, and Society* 10(4): 443–64.

Yoshikawa, H. 2012. *Immigrants Raising Citizens: Undocumented Parents and Their Young Children*. New York: Russell Sage Foundation.

Young, I. 1990. *Justice and the Politics of Difference*. Princeton, NJ: Princeton University Press.

————. 1996. "Communication and the Other: Beyond Deliberative Democracy."
    In *Democracy and Difference: Contesting the Boundaries of the Political,* edited by
    S. Benhabib, 120–36. Princeton, NJ: Princeton University Press.
Zimmer, Ron, B. Gill, K. Booker, S. Lavertu, and J. Witte. 2011. "Do Charter Schools
    'Cream Skim' Students and Increase Racial-Ethnic Segregation?" In *School Choice
    and School Improvement,* edited by M. Berends, M. G. Springer, D. Ballou, and
    H. Walberg, 215–32. Cambridge, MA: Harvard University Press.
Zimmer, Ron, and C. Guarino. 2013. "Is There Empirical Evidence Consistent with the
    Claim That Charter Schools 'Push Out' Low Performing Students?" *Educational
    Evaluation and Policy Analysis* (35)4: 461–80.